THE WENGER CODE

THE WENGER CODE

~

WILL IT SURVIVE THE AGE OF THE OLIGARCH?

By

RICHARD EVANS

GCR BOOKS LIMITED
www.gcrbooks.co.uk

First Edition - 2012

Published by GCR Books Ltd.
Registered in England & Wales. Reg No. 6949535
www.gcrbooks.co.uk
ISBN 978-0-9571443-6-1

Cover design by Steve Wade
stevewade.artwork@hotmail.co.uk

Front and rear cover images © Getty Images

Printed and bound in Great Britain by CPI Group (UK) Ltd, Croydon CR0 4YY

FOR ASHLEY

My very own Gunner

"They do everything here with a touch of class, from the way we play football to off the pitch. They are always doing events, visiting schools, doing charities. It's the Arsenal ethos, helping others, being friendly. Whenever anyone visits the training ground, all the boys make sure they go up to the guest, shake hands, introduce themselves. It's not hard to keep my feet on the ground at a place like Arsenal."

Alex Oxlade-Chamberlain

CONTENTS

INTRODUCTION

Arsenal, ever since the days of Herbert Chapman, have always been different. Stopper centre halves before the genre was understood; the only team with a tube station named after them; white sleeves; under-floor heating in the dressings rooms next to those marble halls at Highbury before World War Two; the art deco elegance of their stadium; a certain, if I may borrow a phrase from the current manager's language, "Je ne sais quoi."

Ever since I was introduced, as a wide-eyed twelve year old to a dripping wet Don Roper as he stepped out of the shower after the winger had scored both goals to defeat Aston Villa in 1951, I was caught up in the spell that has ensnared millions down the years and, with modern media taking the Premiership into households, rich and poor, all over the globe, that spell now enables Arsenal Football Club to call on the support of an unimaginable number of fans – 113 million at the last count in May 2012.

There were 60,000 of them at the Emirates Stadium - a venue that would have made Chapman purr with satisfaction - on 18th August 2012. It was the perfect summer's day for the start of another Premiership season. With at least 80% of the crowd decked out in red and white, it was a vision that sparkled with colour and the hum of anticipation.

Unfortunately the match did not live up to the occasion but neither was it a disaster, this 0-0 draw against Sunderland. It was a match that bedded in the summer's three new signings – Lukas Podolski from Cologne; Olivier Giroud from Montpellier and little Santi Cazorla from Malaga. Podolski, the hugely experienced German international, looked solid and efficient with the promise of better things to come; young Giroud missed a goal he probably would have scored with his eyes shut in France last season while Cazorla began what could be the start of a love affair with the Emirates faithful.

Andrew Longmore, in the Sunday Times, was amongst those impressed by a first look at the Spaniard. "Cazorla is low-slung and quick footed," he wrote. "Every inch the template of a modern Arsenal midfielder. Far from taking time to adapt to the pace of the Premier League, he set the tempo for the afternoon with quick one-twos and real attacking gusto."

From all accounts Cazorla's bouncy, lively style is matched by his off-field personality. His friend Pepe Reina, the Liverpool goalkeeper, nicknamed him Paquirrin. It translates into Fat Boy but if there was any fat on Santi when he arrived in England, it will soon be shed. The Arsenal diet will see to that.

It is his 5 ft 6" which gives the impression of a rotund shape but he has stopped worrying about his height long ago. "It's overstated that smaller, technical players can't do well here," he said. "Being tall isn't what makes you a good footballer."

But on this hot afternoon, Cazorla faded a little later on which was hardly surprising as he had just flown back with the Spanish squad from Puerto Rico. It would take time, something the crowd realized as they filtered away not knowing quite what to make of it. As some filed through the long queues at the Armoury Shop, clutching their replica shirts, or hung around outside gazing at the hundreds of inscriptions on the bricks that make up the paving, there was a murmur of approval for Santi's skills; some chat about Alex Song whose transfer to Barcelona was just being confirmed and, inevitably, the question mark over the two chances missed by Giroud. Would Robin van Persie have taken them?

Van Persie, the latest star and the latest captain to leave Arsenal. The man who, a couple of months before, had come out with a devastating statement about not agreeing with the club's philosophy; a mind-set that would see him sold for £24 million to Manchester United of all teams, with just a year left on his contract.

In saying he did not agree with the direction the club was taking, Van Persie was, in effect, challenging the whole ethos of what I am calling The Wenger Code, the very special and very different philosophy that this tall, spare aesthete from Alsace called Arsene Wenger had brought to the club, and, indeed, to British football, sixteen seasons before.

Harnessing George Graham's water tight defence to his own more vibrant footballing philosophy, Wenger had brought Arsenal instant success with a League and FA Cup double in his second season of 1997-1998 and another double in 2002 and two more FA Cups in 2003 and 2005, sandwiching that extraordinary unbeaten season in the Premiership of 2004.

If Wenger was hailed as a Messiah it was not just because of the titles and the cups. It was because his Code not only cut out the drinking cult; changed diets and training methods and demanded better medical facilities but it produced this mesmerizing brand of beautiful football that turned neutrals into believers and made Arsenal the team everyone wanted to watch.

Gary Neville, who has quickly become a brilliant analyst on Sky Sports, saw the whole introduction of the Wenger Code up close and personal at least a couple of times a season as he guarded Manchester United's right flank and he was talking about it during a pre-amble to United's first game of this season at Goodison Park which they went on to lose 1-0. Poor Robin.

Neville was talking about how the game had changed tactically even since he retired two years before.

"All I had to worry about was the wide man coming down my flank," he said, using all the technological wizardry that Sky developed for his predecessor Andy Gray. "Now the winger comes inside and you have players like Silva, Nasri and Tevez at Manchester City who move about in advanced positions."

Then he added. "The long ball angled in from deep is not seen much any more. Most teams were using it until quite recently except Arsenal who were already playing their way forward with quick passing."

That's what the Wenger Code brought to the Premiership. They were ahead of their time and during the early years Arsene had players with the strength, intelligence and experience to make them invincible for an entire season and pretty hard to beat at other times.

But then the youngsters were asked to take over and the trophies dried up and the exodus began. Patrick Vieira, the commanding captain and midfield general, stroked home the penalty that earned Arsenal the 2005 FA Cup against Manchester United in the shoot-out after a performance that was hardly warranted victory and then left for Juventus.

In many people's opinion he left a year too soon. Maybe Thierry Henry did, too, because he became the next captain to leave the club – the mercurial Frenchman heading for Barcelona where he would have to muck in with a legion of superstars instead of dwarfing his Arsenal team mates by deed and reputation.

Gilberto, the charming and talented Brazilian, also captained the team on occasion and he went, too, to Turkey at the end of the same season that saw Mathieu Flamini and

Alexander Hleb disappear to AC Milan and Barcelona respectively.

And then, of course, came the unkindest cut of all when Cesc Fabregas went home to Barcelona and Samir Nasri jumped ship to cash-rich Manchester City in that badly managed summer of 2011 when Wenger dithered and ended up buying five players as the clock ticked down ludicrously close to midnight at the end of August.

All the while, of course, Arsenal had stopped winning trophies. Oh, they'd been in contention all right, reaching the final of the League Cup in 2007 and 2011, never falling out of the top four in the Premiership, thus ensuring themselves of an extended sequence of qualification for the Champions League in Europe and pulling off some notable and thrilling victories over several of the greatest club teams in the world – Real Madrid, Inter Milan, AC Milan, Barcelona (at least in one leg of the tie) and on numerous occasions against Manchester United, Liverpool and Chelsea. Without question, they were contenders – but they weren't putting trophies in the cabinet and it was trophies that the fans were after.

So were the players, which is why the exodus continued. With Arsenal's restrictive wage structure, it was inevitable that agents, salivating over their commissions, would be egging them on as clubs like Manchester City dangled absurd sums of as much as £200,000 a week in front of their players' noses. But the worrying thing for Arsenal was that it wasn't just about the money.

Fabregas had produced some dazzling performances in a red and white shirt but his trophy cabinet was bare. Not only did the Nou Camp feel like home but there were things to be won in Catalunya or so he thought. But after 49 appearances, several as a sub, and fifteen goals, he had only the Copa del Rey to show for it in his first season in Barcelona colours. They finished second in La Liga – that must have been a familiar feeling – and suffered the ignominy of being beaten in the semi-final of the Champions League by opponents he knew only too well, Chelsea.

But, from all accounts, Cesc enjoyed being back amongst his own folk despite frequent backward glances and actual visits to the club he had left behind. Like Thierry Henry, there is no doubt that Fabregas retains a genuine affection for the Arsenal and the manager who brought him to manhood. You only have to follow his Tweets to realize that.

Nevertheless, fond sentiments could not disguise the fact that two successive Arsenal captains had, in effect, sided with a large number of supporters and lost patience with the Wenger Code. The rumblings of discontent that had started even before the previous summer's fiasco, had grown steadily to a point where a poll conducted by the Gooner Magazine between May and mid-June 2012 suggested that only 27% of supporters answered in the affirmative to this statement: 'Arsene knows and can stay as long as he wants.'

Thirty three per cent wanted him to see out his contract to 2014; while 19% said he should have one more season and another 19% said Wenger's time was up right now.

This contrasted with another poll answered by over 600 members of the Arsenal Supporters Trust. Seventy seven per cent said they still supported the manager despite 38% being unsatisfied with recent performances. When asked about the Board's self-sustaining financial philosophy, which Wenger has backed, only 60% said they approved.

So it is hard to argue with a very rationally laid out article by Peter Le Beau in the Gooner who said, in the issue on sale at the Sunderland game, "......sixteen years after Wenger came to power we find a club in which opinion is extraordinarily divided about whether Arsenal are moving in the right direction – or need a revolution."

Le Beau places himself in the middle and, boring though it may be, I do, too. Instinctively, I support the

Wenger Code of bringing gems like Jack Wilshire through the fine Youth Academy run by Liam Brady and David Court and seeking out teenage talent at other clubs like Fabregas, Kieran Gibbs from Wimbledon and the two Southampton boys, Theo Walcott and Alex Oxlade-Chamberlain.

But with so many established stars leaving, it has never been quite enough to bridge the narrow gap between finishing second or first. As we shall see in the account that follows, Arsenal's failures at certain moments have frequently been miniscule but there is no middle ground between the quick and dead in top class sport. The thinnest of edges is enough to send a batsman back to the pavilion; a ball that hits the underside of the bar and bounces out is not a goal no matter how majestic and deserving the strike. If one factors in what Wenger himself calls financial doping, the team has always been battling against the odds but has managed to stay there or thereabouts over the past few seasons, not merely qualifying for the Champions League but going through to the knock out stages year after year. They have been, and remain, not just one of the top four clubs in England, but, for consistency, amongst the top half dozen in Europe. So the Wenger Code has been tantalizingly close to coming up with the key that would unlock a treasure trove at reasonable cost. What a dream! But so elusive.

And, in this demanding age, there is no patience for coming close. Consistency is not a word that resonates with some supporters whose ambitions for the club are lined with silver. They want Arsenal to win something although, gratifyingly in my view, they are in a minority amongst those asked to look at a bigger picture. Asked which they would prefer: Qualifying for the Champions League or winning the FA Cup or League Cup, 72.9% opted for the former. That, at least, shows an understanding of where the funds come from to sustain that self-sustaining model.

But there are still too many of the brasher, better-heeled brigade who came on board when Wenger started winning things for the club at a swanky new stadium with its corporate boxes because it was seen as the chic thing to do. As long as Arsenal were winning they had something to boast about. To be fair everyone likes to be associated with success but some supporters need to be reminded than no team, not even Arsenal, have a divine right to win things.

The counter argument to the self-sustaining model is put forward by the Uzbek multi-billionaire Alisher Usmanov who, at the last count owned 29.72 % of Arsenal's shares but was still not welcome to take a seat on the Board. David Dein, the club's former mover, shaker, Vice Chairman and doer of deals, was Chairman of Usmanov's Red and White Holdings for a while after he was kicked off the Arsenal Board and shares approximately the same philosophy.

"Arsenal need the best available players on the field," says Dein, who used to talk with his friend Arsene and then go out and find them.

Life is not so simple now. Arsenal are in grave danger of becoming a feeder club to those enterprises owned by Russian or Middle Eastern billionaires and that, in the view of many supporters, is demeaning.

But Wenger seems acutely aware of it and was discussing the problem more openly than usual after the draw against Sunderland.

Responding to inevitable questions about Van Persie's departure that very week, Wenger said, "Maybe the critics are right, maybe they are wrong. I don't know. But it is true last year, in every game, Robin found something special. I never denied we lost a world class player. He's very difficult to replace."

The situation was not being helped by the fact that Alex Song was in the process of moving to Barcelona as he spoke.

"We make players here," said the designer of dreams with a resigned look clouding his long, drawn features. "All those who have left were made here, or made a name here or came here very young. Fabregas, Clichy, Adebayor, Henry, Nasri. Song came at seventeen."

And those were names he could just pluck off the top of his head. The stars, if you like. Look around the Premiership and the Championship and the Football League and you will find an amazing number of teams that include players who began their careers at Arsenal but lacked that extra special something required to satisfy Wenger's standards.

A few years ago I took my son Ashley, who plays a lot of school soccer in Richmond, Virginia, to a couple of training sessions at Hale End where Arsenal have their Junior Academy. The speed and skill of the nine and ten year olds Ashley found himself playing with was astounding. Yet no more than one per cent will become an Arsenal first team regular.

And so many have tried and almost got there. Jay Simpson scored for Hull City in the first match of this season. Seb Larsson was playing for Sunderland against his old club. Steve Sidwell scored a penalty for Fulham who would have had Philippe Senderos in defence if he had been fit. Anthony Stokes at Celtic; Jerome Thomas at West Brom; Matthew Upson at Stoke City, Matthew Connolly and Armand Traore at QPR; Gavin Hoyte starting a new career at Dagenham and, surprisingly, Kyle Bartley being allowed to make a permanent move to Swansea City. And the list could continue.

"I think part of our club is to influence people's lives in a positive way," Wenger added. "But it doesn't always happen."

He was being melancholy. The vast majority of youngsters who have flirted with first team football at Arsenal and moved on have had productive careers. Which is great but it is, of course, the big names that catch the attention of the media and fascinate the fans. Especially when they go off somewhere in search of……..what?

"I don't think it is linked at all with winning something or always about money," Wenger said before adding mysteriously, "Every case is individual and maybe one day I will explain everything."

What this fascinating individual may need to explain is the extent to which he found a different key for one essential part of his Code and realised that he needed some more seasoned players to add some backbone to the tender shoots he was nurturing. Unless he reveals all in what would be a spell-binding autobiography, we may never know to what extent Wenger has hidden behind his team's youth as he tried, with great skill and vision, to re-produce the triumphs of his early years in North London.

"You must remember, we are so young," was a phrase he uttered time and time again towards the end of the last decade. And they were. In 2008, the average age of the squad was 22.06, kindergarten stuff compared with most of their rivals. At the start of the 2011-2012 season the average age had risen to 24.8 but that still made Wenger's kids the youngest squad in the Premiership.

And he believed in them. He was like some kindly but combustibly jealous uncle; nursing his flock; never saying a word against them in public; never seeing their transgressions on the field; fighting their corner furiously with officialdom. It was admirable in so many ways – not least because the grateful youngsters felt protected – but it also gave the media the chance to turn this very serious man into a figure of fun. Jokes about spectacles became very boring.

Like football managers, football correspondents can make errors of judgment which is hardly surprising as they are required to produce opinions of great insight right on the button. Henry Winter of the Daily Telegraph is a wonderful wordsmith on deadline but he is forever jumping on Arsenal's flaws, especially their manager.

Trawling back through some cuttings – a nasty thing to do to a newspaperman as opposed to an author – I came up with this gem from Winter, written in April 2001, when he felt that Wenger had lost his way after guiding Arsenal to the League and Cup double in 1998. "When it comes to the Premiership, Wenger has his balance wrong. The chemistry remains flawed. Next season's challenge to (Manchester) United may come from Elland Road (Leeds United) and Anfield (Liverpool) unless Wenger invests intelligently and throws off his inferiority complex."

Apparently he did both because Arsenal promptly did the double – again. Where Winter got the idea that Wenger had an inferiority complex I'm not quite sure. And there hadn't been much investment. David Seaman, Patrick Vieira, Robert Pires, Freddie Ljungberg, Thierry Henry, Ray Parlour and Dennis Bergkamp led them to the title, seven points clear of Liverpool. And they had all been there the year before.

So Winter got that one wrong but he was nearer the mark ten years later when he had more cause to try and dissect Arsenal's problems. Winter said it was Wenger himself who needed to change. "Wenger needs to open his eyes, finally seeing his own and his team's faults."

He quoted the text that was doing the rounds amongst the disgruntled. "From In Arsene We Trust to In Arsene We Rust."

Harsh – and there was less of that kind of talk by the time Wenger dug his team out of an early grave in September 2011 and somehow lifted them to a third place finish. It wasn't Arsene's greatest achievement but it was up there.

With Champions League football assured once again and replacements for Van Persie already signed just in case he really did move on, Wenger was able to enjoy a less fretful and frenetic summer than twelve months before. But that could not hide the fact that Arsenal had suffered two of their most frustrating seasons since his arrival in 1998.

Why and how? I certainly don't have the answers because, firstly I am not a coach and secondly one of the best in the business, a certain Arsene Wenger, is not absolutely certain he knows himself.

So, to find an outlet for my frustration, I tied my Arsenal scarf around my neck and took a detailed look at the highs and lows and ultimate failures of the last two campaigns. Unashamedly I looked at them through the lens of an Arsenal fan. Because this book is written for all of you.

1

IRONY

The Barbarians were at the gates as Arsenal flew off to Trieste for the second leg of their Champions League qualifier in August 2011. Under siege from a press corps which had been feasting off six months of hell for Arsene Wenger and his team, they were to play Udinese Calcio, a club from the ancient city of Udine, just north of Trieste, whose history might have increased the shivers down supporters' spines had they read it.

The first signs of a settlement appeared in about 430 AD when Attila the Hun wanted a hill built so he could have a vantage point for his campaign against Aquileia. So he ordered his soldiers to fill their helmets and shields with earth and had them build one. Many people thought this journey a hill too steep for Arsenal in any case, without the ghost of Attila lingering amidst the sticky air of a suffocatingly hot night.

But it was not some ancient warrior Arsenal had to worry about. They laid his ghost with a fine display, beating Udinese 2-1 on the night, (3-1 on aggregate) after Wojciech Szczesny had produced a terrific save from an Antonio di Natale penalty and so ensured participation in the

Champions League for the 15th straight season – an astounding achievement by anyone's standards.

No, it was on their return to the UK that Arsenal ran into their own, very much alive, Attila in the form of Sir Alex Ferguson and his marauding hordes who inhabit Old Trafford. There, Wenger's men were truly sacked, humiliated and laid to waste as Manchester United ran up a score-line than will live in infamy – 8-2.

Of course, there were mitigating circumstances but they were largely ignored as the media did its best to ram that incredible score down Wenger's throat. It was, as always, the only statistic that mattered but most Arsenal fans would have grabbed at these stats before the match – two goals (Arsenal hadn't scored twice at Old Trafford since the inception of the Premier League in 1992) five corners to United's three and thirteen shots on target, only two less than the Red Devils. Trouble was, their's went in.

There were moments, in fact, when Arsenal played quite well which was a miracle in itself because, for a variety of reasons having to do, almost in equal measure, with sheer bad luck and their own stupidity, Arsenal were forced to field a heavily depleted side. Alex Song, Gervinho and Frimpong were suspended; Kieran Gibbs, Jack Wilshere, and Abou Diaby were injured and then, to make quite sure Wenger understood how ridiculously fates could conspire against him, Thomas Vermaelen failed a fitness test on the morning of the match and Bacary Sagna was taken ill two days before. That meant Laurent Koscielny had to be hauled off the treatment table and pressed into action as Arsenal's only first choice defender apart from Wojciech Szczesny.

And even then Arsenal should have drawn level at 1-1 when Robin van Persie missed a penalty and should have closed the gap to 3-2 when Van Persie had the goal at his mercy but hurried his shot and allowed the suspect David de Gea to pull off a fine save. So Arsenal could have scored four times. Not much compensation when Man U scored eight.

The fall out, of course, was considerable. The media and Tim Payton of the Arsenal Supporters Trust were vociferous in their demands for change, some saying that Wenger had to buy with the transfer deadline looming. But Payton went further. In an article in the Independent, Payton wrote, "The club need to re-think their "self-sustaining" business model. This doesn't mean an unchecked sugar-daddy approach but it does mean reviewing options to bridge the gap (with Man City and Chelsea) such as paying down the remaining debt or undertaking a rights issue."

In a direct challenge to the Wenger Code, Payton went on to say that 70% of Arsenal supporters felt that Wenger's football philosophy had taken too much precedence over securing football success. It was a natural reaction but a close analysis of the previous season reveals just how close Arsenal were to proving that the Wenger Code could work. He was not fantasizing when he said "we were so close" at numerous press conferences. They were. One fraction-of-second slip in the Carling Cup final; hitting the woodwork 19 times in the Premiership, any half dozen of which could have turned draws into wins or defeats into draws; that split second between the referee's whistle blowing and Robin van Persie kicking the ball out in Barcelona – too many happenings that made a mockery of the notion that there are laws of probability. The improbable kept on happening to Arsenal with a consistency that defied belief.

Nevertheless even allowing for the media's inevitable delight in stoking a bad angle in a dramatic story, Arsenal, in late August 2011, were teetering on the edge of a full blown crisis. Wenger, whenever he appeared in public, looked haggard. Originally, he had talked about settling the in-coming transfers by the end of July. But that deadline was long gone.

"It has been the most disturbed pre-season I have

ever had," said a manager who almost never gives one-to-one interviews but is very open with his thoughts in general press conference. "When I go to hell one day, it will be less painful for me than for you because I'm used to suffering."

It was said with just a touch of submerged humour but it revealed the extent of Wenger's pain.

The very day the team flew to Italy to face Udinese, Samir Nasri was presenting himself in Manchester as City's latest example of what money was doing to the game of football. Nasri, plucked from Marseille four seasons before, had been Arsenal's best player in the first half of the previous season but now he had been lured away by wages which were rumoured to be £180,000 a week – about £80,000 more than Arsenal were offering him for a new contract. Instead of wittering on about Manchester City being "a team for the future" it would have been nice if Nasri had said simply, "£80,000 a week is a lot of money to turn down." Which it is.

A week before Nasri's departure, Arsenal had lost its captain for somewhat different reasons. Cesc Fabregas had nearly re-joined his boyhood club, Barcelona, the previous season and now Wenger was forced to bow to the inevitable. Harried and pushed by an incessant cacophony of quotes coming from the Catalans, headed by such Barca players as Puyol and Iniesta, Arsenal finally put its signature on a deal that let this magical midfielder go for £35 million – at least five million less than his real worth in an ever escalating transfer market. But this was not a question of a player being dazzled by dollars. It appeared that Fabregas was even willing to accept less than Barcelona's original offer in wages so that he could return to his home town. Rare though it might be in this hard-nosed commercial world, this really was a matter of the heart.

Not that Arsenal fans found any consolation in that although, in the end, there was a sense of relief that Cesc had packed his bags. The reasons were twofold. Firstly, his mind would never be 100% on the job of playing for Arsenal for another season and, secondly, his dodgy hamstrings might continue to let him down as consistently as they had in the previous twelve months.

But no club can lose its two playmakers, both judged to be amongst the best in the world, and pretend that it was anything less than a shocking blow to the team's solar plexus.

Some months later, when things had turned around quicker than anyone at Arsenal dared imagine at the time, Laurent Koscielny, gave a fascinating interview to the magazine France Football. When a player speaks in his native tongue, a different personality often emerges and Koscielny certainly revealed himself as a thinking, articulate footballer on this occasion.

"The beginning of the season was a catastrophe," he admitted. "We'd lost players who were key to our system. We recruited late and it took a while to gel. We were whopped at Old Trafford. Everyone thought we were dead and buried. But you don't lose your footballing ability just like that. It can happen that a grain of sand falls into the machine and the machine stalls. Then you start to have doubts about your qualities, your club, your coach, everything."

In the British media, the above quote was presented as "Koscielny doubted Wenger" but Laurent went on to suggest that the players were examining themselves every bit as much as their manager.

"We had to put the house back in order. And everyone did their bit. The squad wasn't giving enough for the club. We got back to work. We told each other things that needed to be told."

Unhappily, they didn't tell each other enough things quickly enough. "Don't retaliate needlessly" being one of them.

After the desperate happenings of those harrowing

months in the spring when everything slipped from Arsenal's grasp, the team returned from a first-ever pre-season tour to the Far East and promptly set about shooting themselves in the foot all over again.

While certain players have to carry the blame, the computerised fixture list showed just how much fates were conspiring against the club when it decreed that a visit to Newcastle of all places would be the first business on the new season's agenda; followed by a home game against Liverpool and then a visit to Old Trafford. It would have been tough under any circumstances but Joey Barton ensured that it would get tougher still. How? Just by being Joey Barton. We will look at the havoc he caused during that amazing 4-4 come back from 0-4 down at St James' Park six months before later on but, by the time Arsenal had struggled out of town clutching a 0-0 draw he had done it again. Incredibly, after two consecutive matches at St James' Barton had been directly involved with three Arsenal players receiving red cards (either instant or delayed) while he himself had managed to stay on the pitch. That may be an achievement unmatched in the history of English football.

It had been Abou Diaby's illegal reaction to his dangerously heavy tackle that had seen the tall midfielder sent off in the first encounter and, with that incident no doubt playing on his mind, Alex Song, who shouldn't have been so stupid, put his foot down on Barton's prone leg not long after the new season had opened. The referee missed it but, of course, the cameras didn't so the Premiership review board were able to ban Song for three games because the officials had taken no action at the time.

But worse was to follow. Gervinho, Arsenal's new signing from Lille who had been causing the Magpies' defence a few problems, was chasing a ball in the penalty area when Cheik Tiote's boot caught his foot. It was a feint touch but Gervinho went down. The crowd roared in disapproval because it appeared that Gervinho had dived.

Replays proved this to be untrue but Barton decided to act on "behalf of his team mates and all those great fans who did not deserve to be cheated" (a new high in sanctimonious claptrap, I thought) and proceeded to reach down with two hands and jerk Gervinho to his feet. Is it or is it not a red card offense if you lay hands aggressively on another player? This was certainly aggressive but before the ref could do anything all hell broke loose and a lot of handbags were flying around. A crowd of players jostled around Barton and Gervinho, now on his feet, reached around the outside of them and slapped the side of Barton's head. The blow was no harder than one might expect an exasperated mother to deliver to a disobedient child. But Barton, of course, went down as if he had been swiped by a cricket bat. Afterwards he had the gall – decency...take your pick – to admit that he went down "easily". So easily that the gullible referee sent off Gervinho. Barton? A yellow. So, let's take a look at this: initiating an incident aggressively with two hands is, apparently, a lesser offense than retaliating in relatively mild fashion with one. Why do professional and, presumably, intelligent officials, go on making such as ass of the rules?

So Arsenal, once again, were down to ten men but this time the defence – the much maligned defence of Sagna, Koscielny, Vermaelen and Gibbs (now in the team for the departed Gael Clichy – to Man City, of course) – held firm. However, Arsenal were the losers. Two key players out for three matches, including that trip to Man U.

But worse was to follow. Young Frimpong, who had missed the whole of the previous season, with a knee injury, had been showing just what kind of prospect he is with some sterling displays in pre-season friendlies and was drafted into the side against Liverpool at the Emirates on August 20th in place of Song. For much of the first half, Song was hardly missed. Arsenal were far from being at their smooth-passing best but one of the highlights had been Frimpong's sudden surge into the Liverpool half which ended with a rasping drive that missed Reina's right hand post by no more than a yard.

However – say something good about Arsenal and there's usually a 'however' – Frimpong had shown his immaturity in the 8th minute by delaying a Liverpool throw and getting booked. So when his judgment deserted him again in the 69th minute, showing studs to Lucas Leiva with a nasty lunge, the ref had no option. Frimpong was off and now Arsenal had lost its two top holding midfielders.

Oh, and did I forget to mention? Jack Wilshere was injured. And it was to prove a serious one. Some bone damage on the ankle meant that the young man who had been ear-marked as the lynchpin of England's midfield, let alone Arsenal's, for years to come, would be hobbling around for days in an orthopedic boot. After numerous scans, he was told to rest it for two months. So no Wilshere until November was the first prognosis although that turned out to be tragically optimistic. Who could have imagined that Jack would not be back until the following autumn? The previous year the club had lost Van Persie until Christmas and Vermaelan for the entire season and now, believe it or not, the Belgian would be sidelined again at the beginning of September for an ankle operation. Nothing too serious, they said. Just out for six weeks. Other clubs suffer long term injuries. Arsenal just seem to suffer them more consistently. To the above just add the horrendous bone-breaking, ligament-tearing tackles that did for Diaby, Eduardo and Aaron Ramsey, not to mention the broken leg suffered by Nasri in pre-season training in 2009. It's a long list.

The clamour for Wenger to dive into the transfer market became a drum beat as every pundit drew up lists of players the manager should buy. One thing was clear: Wenger had ten days between the Old Trafford debacle and the end of the transfer window to do something to assuage the anxiety and, in some cases, the sheer fury of Arsenal fans. I would guess that if one had a taken a straw poll amongst the Arsenal faithful during that week in August most would have guessed at Wenger signing two or three more players. Amazingly, he found five.

And, more than the actual number, possibly the most amazing aspect of his choices were their ages. None under 26. Fans had been screaming for experienced players who could walk straight into the Premier League and, finally, it seemed that Wenger had got the message. But had he gone too far the other way? Had the Wenger Code got muddled in the frantic need to make up for the procrastination of the previous weeks? Had he ended up with players past their prime? Had he simply been forced to grab what he could get? These were the new questions buzzing around North London as deadline day approached and everything seemed to hang on a knife edge.

Watching the ticker-tape on the BBC website or scrolling down the tweets from informed people like Young Guns, the drama built hour by hour. Names like Gary Cahill, Phil Jagielka and Christopher Samba were still on the radar but no one could confirm a safe landing.

First in was Ju-Young Park from Monaco, a 26-year-old striker who had recently taken over the captaincy of South Korea. That signing seemed to entail some spy-novel negotiations with Park vanishing from his hotel room in Lille where he had been on the point of signing for Gervinho's old club. Wails of protest from the Lille hierarchy but the bird had flown.

Then news came through that Per Mertesacker was on his way from Werder Bremen. A veteran German international of 27 – that took care of the centre back problem, or so one hoped. Then it was the Brazilian Andre Santos to give Gibbs some competition for the left-back position. Santos came from Fenerbahce in Turkey and was 28.

The final drama involved replacements for the two departed midfielders. First, we heard that Mikel Arteta was about to sign from Everton. Then the deal was off and it was going to be Yossi Benayoun on loan from Chelsea. Then, apparently, Arteta told his agent to back off and accept a lower wage more in line with Arsenal's pay restrictions. So Arteta it was as the clock moved towards the 11.00 pm cut-off on the Wednesday night. But, to many people's surprise, that did not knock Benayoun out of the picture. With minutes to go, he came, too. So Arteta, at 28, and Benayoun, at 31, became two of Wenger's most unusual signings – veterans whose best football might have been behind them but who would silence those critics who had been calling for experienced campaigners.

But, of course, as we shall see the ship had not been righted. It was still listing and leaking goals. More of that to come. But first let's reflect a little on what had gone before and see if any of it made any sense.

2

IT COULD HAVE BEEN DIFFERENT

Arsene Wenger's mantra during pre-season press conferences as the 2011-2012 campaign dawned was "We were so close, so close."

The Arsenal manager was referring to the frequently weird and barely comprehensible series of misfortunes that had seen the club fall from a position of high promise at the end of January 2011 (the only club in Britain still in contention for four trophies at that stage) to an ignominious fourth place finish in the Premiership and no trophies by May.

Wenger's hair was whiter but still lustrous, as he faced the cameras. It was a wonder it hadn't fallen out. "The summer has been hell," he admitted, referring as much to the interminable wrangling over transfers as to the actual collapse of so many dreams on the playing field. It was a minor miracle that he had retained his sanity. Here was a man who lived, breathed and dreamt football to a point far beyond obsession and who had seen those dreams unravel in a fashion that contained so many improbables as to defy the laws of what can reasonably be expected to happen.

I don't want to use the word luck while trying to describe what went on during that hair-tearing, hand-wringing campaign of 'If onlys' because Arsenal used to be called Lucky Arsenal in by-gone days and to call them unlucky now would be pathetic. But there is supposed to be a law of probability and it was almost impossible to believe that so many improbable things occurred to dismantle a beautifully constructed footballing machine to the extent that they did.

But late in the summer an extraordinary set of statistics were released by a freelance journalist called Tim Long which backed up Wenger's assertion that "we were so close" to an amazing degree. Long had poured through every Premiership match of 2010-2011 and logged every decision by a referee that, after reviewing the video tape, had proved to be incorrect. There were 713 of them.

Now you are always going to get dubious decisions from officials no matter how much technological assistance you give them and I am not totally unsympathetic to those who say that human error is part of sport and we should get on with it. Nevertheless, Long's findings were fascinating because they backed up what two managers had been feeling frequently during the season – namely that the old adage that mistakes even up was just not happening in their case. One was Ian Holloway, who was bemoaning Blackpool's fate from the roof tops virtually every time the whistle blew against his talented team and the other was Wenger who, with one or two exceptions, was somewhat more restrained.

Long's findings were these: If all refereeing errors had been eradicated Arsenal would have finished second behind Manchester United on goal difference with Chelsea third and Manchester City fourth while Blackpool and Birmingham City should have stayed up in place of Wigan and Wolves.

At the top of the table, the points added or deducted were as follows:

Man U	-9
Arsenal	+3
Chelsea	-5
Man City	-7.

With those revisions, Man U and Arsenal would have finished with 71 points each.

Long then produced another table in which he took the whole exercise a little further by applying the laws of probability to each wrong decision and making an educated guess as to what would have happened next. He insists he has no bias but obviously opinions here would vary. However his top of the table formations remained unchanged except for the fact that Man U would have won by five clear points with 77 points to Arsenal's 72. Chelsea would have had 70 and Man City 62.

Some critics rubbished the whole exercise, saying it was pointless and telling Long to get real. But what it did do was show up the huge influence referees have on the outcome of matches and the historical fate of clubs. Finishing second instead or fourth makes a big difference – Man City would have had to qualify for last season's Champions League instead of Arsenal, for instance – but that pales against the enormity of staying up or getting relegated.

Long, needless to say, is an advocate of more technology. "The fact is too many important decisions are being called incorrectly and any one of them could have a monumental effect on a club. In the modern day game with so much on the line that surely cannot be allowed to continue."

I tend to agree with him and if his exercise puts more pressure on FIFA to install goal line cameras inside goal posts as a minimal first step – off-side technology should follow – then Long will have done the game a great service.

Obviously his findings were both satisfying and frustrating for those wearing an Arsenal hat and, looking at them through a Gooner prism, not without error. While acknowledging that Van Persie had a goal disallowed for off-side against Sunderland, he makes no mention of the fact that Arshavin was pushed in the back while clear through on goal and in the act of shooting in the same match. Nor did he mention the referee ignoring Nolan pushing Diaby in the chest after the Arsenal midfielder had been red carded at Newcastle. That, surely, was a yellow card offense at the least and would have resulted in a second yellow when the Newcastle captain grabbed Szczesny in a headlock after the Magpies had started their unlikely come back from 0-4 down. With ten men against ten, it is hard to believe the score would have ended 4-4.

So that could have given Arsenal two more points in Long's table and, therefore, the title! Lovely to dream but you can only return to reality and start asking questions. They are almost endless. And searching for answers leaves you grasping for a thread of logic; leaves you wondering how improbability can outscore probability with such relentless persistence.

Apparently it can because it has kept on happening in Arsenal's recent history. Every team makes mistakes and has players that are prone to making mistakes. But it is not often that a team's icons – the very best players to have appeared in their respective positions for the club – are the ones whose errors change the club's history for the worse.

That, unhappily, is what happened as far as David Seaman, Dennis Bergkamp, Thierry Henry and Cesc Fabregas are concerned. The first three were involved in errors that were absolutely definitive. Fabregas, in the season 2010-2011, made a couple that could have changed the course of that campaign if some sort of logic had followed.

Take Seaman. Many people's choice as Arsenal's best ever goalkeeper. But he was off his line – reasonably so – when Nayim took an outrageous punt from nearly 40 yards out in the Cup Winners Cup Final at the Parc des Princes in

Paris in 1995 and watched it sail over Seaman's head and into the net. The Arsenal keeper made such a good job of back peddling that, at the last gasp, there was barely enough room for the ball to pass between Seaman's upstretched hand and the cross bar. The shot was so perfect as to be unrepeatable. So Seaman was desperately unlucky – but it was still his mistake. And Arsenal lost to Real Zaragoza 2-1.

In 1999, Arsenal were awarded a penalty against Manchester United in the FA Cup semi-final. There were about two minutes left to play when Dennis Bergkamp walked up to take it. Even though he had missed a spot kick a couple of weeks earlier, the odds on the Dutch maestro doing so again were long – very long. Few people in the world have been able to kick a football with greater accuracy than Bergkamp. But, unbelievably, he repeated his earlier mistake, and the goalie made a comfortable save. In extra time Ryan Giggs went off on his amazing run to score the best goal of his career and it was Man U who went through to play Newcastle United in the final. Of course, they won – as Arsenal almost certainly would have done – and so became the first club ever to win three trophies in one season. Bergkamp's miss re-wrote footballing history.

In 2006, Arsenal were playing Barcelona in their first ever Champions League final, again in Paris, but this time at the Stade de France. Thierry Henry had grown up nearby in the northern suburb of St Denis. But it was not to be a happy homecoming. With Arsenal leading against all the odds – Sol Campbell having scored after Jens Lehmann was dismissed very early on – Henry was put clear with only the goalkeeper to beat in the 64th minute. How often does the goalie come out on top when faced with Henry bearing down on him? Not often but Victor Valdes did that night. Henry's side-footed shot was blocked and a cast iron chance to put Arsenal 2-0 up was gone. As thunder clouds unleashed a torrential downpour from a black Parisian sky, Barcelona scored twice late in the second half and deprived Arsenal of a trophy that should have been theirs because, even with ten men, they had looked the better team for much of the contest.

What makes an intelligent world class player do something really silly? I wish I knew the answer but even if you asked Cesc Fabregas why he jumped with both arms up above his waist when standing in his own penalty area for a free kick he might not be able to give you an answer. But it happened and it happened against, of all people, Tottenham Hotspur. Arsenal had run rings round their old enemy during the first half at the Emirates. There were a lot of happy and slightly smug faces in the bar at half time. Spurs hadn't beaten the Gunners on Arsenal territory for 17 years and surely that was not going to change.

But Gareth Bale scored a good goal in the 50th minute and then Spurs were awarded a free kick a few yards outside the Arsenal penalty area on the left hand side. Fabregas was on the end of the wall and as Van der Vaart kicked he jumped with a hand covering his face. Of course the ball hit his hand. Dead centre. Penalty. Van der Vaart scored and Tottenham were 2-2. Suddenly it was panic stations. Harry Redknapp's men grew in confidence, went for the jugular and found it in the 85th minute as Van der Vaart provided the perfect cross for the big defender Younes Kaboul to glance in a delicately placed header. Three points chucked away. But if Fabregas had kept his arms down.........

The captain was involved in an inexplicable decision at the Nou Camp, too. Arsenal, of course, had silenced the critics to a man by defeating Barcelona at the Emirates on 16th February, coming back from 1-0 down with two superb goals, first from Van Persie and then Arshavin who hit one of his crackers – a first time shot from Nasri's pin-point cross.

The previous season, Arsenal had gone to the Nou Camp having drawn at home so this was an even better opportunity and despite the fact that the Catalan maestros had just as much possession in the first half hour as they had at the Emirates, the defence held firm, despite the fact that Szczesny had been forced to hand over to Almunia after tearing a finger ligament with no more than 15 minutes gone. Almunia, in fact, proceeded to play one of his best games for Arsenal which was an irony in itself considering how poorly he had been regarded in his native Spain.

But the bigger irony came in the third minute of first half injury time. The score, miraculously it seemed, was still 0-0 which meant Arsenal were going through. But all that changed as a result of the decision Fabregas made on the edge on his own penalty area. He tried a back pass. Right there with all those Barcelona forwards buzzing around him, ready to snap up any unconsidered morsel on offer. This was unconsidered, all right, and a little morsel turned into a great big goal as Iniesta pounced and fed Messi. No more assistance required. The little genius pulled the ball down as if it was on a string and slotted past Almunia.

Fabregas must have wanted to descend into the bowels of the stadium and hide. This was the match he had been desperate to play in, partially because of what it meant to Arsenal but also because he wanted to show off his wares to his home town fans and impress a club he wanted to join.

In a very revealing interview several weeks later, Cesc admitted that he should never have played. "After 12 minutes I knew I wasn't fit but I was too embarrassed to come off that early."

How ironic was that? Here was the Arsenal captain, having announced to everyone's joy and relief, that he was fit to play in possibly the most important game of the season only to discover that he was nothing of the sort. And once he was on the pitch he actually became a negative factor by setting up Barcelona's only first half goal for them. Why he stayed on until the 76th minute is a mystery because he contributed little.

Van Persie had also been a serious injury doubt before the match and he, too, became a liability by getting himself booked in a little fit of temper in the first half and then kicking the ball away one second – one actual second – after the referee, Massimo Busacca, had blown for off-side and getting himself sent off. Arsenal, having been presented with an own goal by Sergio Busquets' header from a good Nasri corner, were 1-1 at the time. In other words they were still going through. But, of course, reduced to ten men it was only a matter of time before Barcelona scored two more goals, one a penalty. Even then a beautifully weighted pass from the impressive Jack Wilshere landed right in front Nicklas Bendtner as the forward roared through the middle but the Dane's feet were wrong and instead of a gentle touch with the outside of his boot to give him scoring room, he let the ball bobble to his left and the chance was gone. Had he scored Arsenal would have been poised to qualify for the next round once more.

So a Cup Winners Cup, an FA Cup and a Champions League title plus a famous Champions League win were all plucked from Arsenal's grasp as a result of four of their greatest players making errors at definitive moments. Improbable? Of course but not more so than the manner in which rather less great players like Tiote, Rose, Bentley and Perisic for Borussia Dortmund last season, have produced performances or one-off moments of brilliance that they have never repeated against any other team. And that doesn't include a bevy of goalkeepers from Maik Taylor of Birmingham City to West Ham's Robert Green having blinders as soon as they see red and white shirts in front of them. So, in the improbability stakes, Arsenal always seem to lose out both ways

Finding a reason why has become an annual task for all those scribes and commentators whose job it is to come up with rational answers for what happens on a football pitch. But, if truth be told, it is a futile occupation because so much of what happens on a football pitch is bizarre (good word, that, it's French) irrational, illogical and just downright crazy.

Football is a choreographed game defined by chaos. I was taken to a ballet a few months ago and, listening to my lady, Gayle, who knows about these things, I was told that every step, every tiny step, is choreographed and rehearsed down to the last detail. And, then, a few weeks later, a commercial appeared on American television, linking ballet and soccer, as they call it. Since then, Arsenal themselves have gone further. Responding to a request from their sponsor Citroen to film a commercial for the new DS5, Szczesny, Song, Sagna and Oxlade-Chamberlain turned up at the National Ballet to do a photo shoot with leading ballerinas. All the players were impressed by the suppleness and muscle strength required to strike balletic poses. The speed of movement, the athleticism, the twirling, swirling figures that are so obvious in Swan Lake can also be caught, if you watch in slow motion, as players go up for a corner. You'd be surprised, even the likes of Djourou can be caught in a balletic pose! Szczesny had done a bit of ballroom dancing but Song was a novice and had to put up with some rather obvious jokes about shooting over the barre.

There is no question that both disciplines demand a level of fitness and, especially in ballet, a suppleness that is far beyond the capability of the average person. But, of course, the differences are stark – as stark as the basic difference between theatre and sport. In one, you know the ending and the other you don't. But that does not mean football is not choreographed. Not, one has to admit, to the same degree as it is in the grid-iron game in the States but it is planned to a greater extent than the casual follower might have imagined before Andy Gray started using his magnetic board on Sky TV – a job which Stewart Robson does with such clarity on the Arsenal web-site now.

Managers spend weeks in pre-season marshalling their forces, drumming into each player the exact position that he needs to be in so as to maximize the strength of particular players and particular patterns of play. It is called keeping your shape and apparently Steve Bould, a member of the club's famous Tony Adams-led backline who has now taken over from Pat Rice as assistant first team coach, is a stickler for 'shape'.

Playing a high line to catch the opposition off-side or to press them onto the defensive requires lock-in concentration for the back four that can weary the brain as much as this non-stop, all action sport wearies the body. And sometimes it comes down to an inch – with Arsenal the margins seldom seem to be any bigger. Remember the Carling Cup final of 2007? Arsenal's very young team, were leading Chelsea's old sweats 1-0 thanks to Theo Walcott's coolly taken goal from Abou Diaby's pass. And then Philippe Senderos played Didier Drogba on-side. By how much? Take a look at the replays. By the length of his heel. Half a step forward and he would have played Drogba off-side and the first Chelsea goal would not have been scored. Would Arsenal have won? It was a tall ask but as Chelsea only ended up with a 2-1 advantage anything could have happened.

But, mostly, the discipline is there during regular bouts of play. Wilshere finds his path blocked going forward so he barely has to look before swinging a lateral pass out to Sagna who, he knows, will be waiting out there on the right hand touchline to take the pass. Especially with Arsenal, there is a symmetrical flow to their forward movement that is as fluid as it is pre-planned. Hours on the training pitch get players used to the idea that they can roam; that Walcott and Arshavin or, now, Gervinho, can suddenly switch wings and have all the other pieces fall into place. But as soon as play moves into the penalty box everything speeds up and no amount of pre-planning can account for the flailing foot; the outstretched leg or the sly shoulder barge. And when the corner comes in, then chaos really does reign as attackers race around, jockeying for position, desperately trying to lose their markers amidst flying limbs and goalkeepers' grasping gloves.

And, frequently, what happens next makes little sense. In a blur of unchoreographed movement the ball can find its way into the net off head, heel, undetected elbow or knee (ask poor Alex Song). Unless he, himself is blatantly at fault, the goalkeeper will rail at his defence but it is really all about being tiny fractions of a second quicker to the ball. If your toe poke or header or wild slash flies inches inside the post, you are a hero and will be acclaimed as such in huge headlines in the next day's paper's or on the internet in ten seconds. But if your effort hits the woodwork, then the score stays the same and the effort is quickly forgotten. Arsenal hit the woodwork 21 times in 2010-2011, an agonizing miss ratio only equalled by Chelsea. If 20% of those shots had been two inches lower or to the left or right, the Gunners would most certainly have won something and it would probably have been the Premier League. The same, of course, is true of Chelsea. So does missing by two or three inches 21 times make Arsenal that much worse than Man U? The fact that Arsenal got themselves into a position to score so often proves how dominant they were for so much of so many matches.

Newcastle United, who had so much input into Arsenal's season, had one chance at the Emirates and Andy Carroll scored. Arsenal had at least half a dozen and hit the woodwork three times but lost 1-0. On one occasion, Theo Walcott left a valiant Newcastle defence standing and hit the cross bar. Two inches lower and it would have been 1-1. Does that kind of margin make Newcastle a better side than Arsenal? Hardly but it's all about scoring goals, isn't it? In the greater scheme of things that's all that matters. Which is why I can never understand why Peter Crouch isn't always picked for England. He scores far more goals than anyone else who is selected so how on earth can he be kept out? It was the same argument with David Beckham. When he played he either made or scored more goals than anyone else. So why the debate?

As far as the Gunners are concerned, it would be nice if some of this made sense. But nothing about Arsenal over these past six seasons has been normal, rational, logical or has gone remotely according to plan. And there has been a plan, a great plan. It has been Arsene Wenger's plan, part of his broad Code, to bring the most talented young group of players in the country through to the first team while buying very frugally in the transfer market when absolutely necessary. And he has done it brilliantly.

The young players from Cesc Fabregas to Jack Wilshere are amongst the most admired and sought after in the world. Most of the money spent has been spent well. Bacary Sagna from Auxerre for £6 million; Samir Nasri from Marseille for £15 million; Thomas Vermaelen from Ajax for £10 million. And, yes, Andrey Arshavin from St Petersburg for £15m. Go back to signings secured at the early stages of players' careers, Robin van Persie (£2.7 million); Mathieu Flamini (£1 million) and the experienced Gilberto (£4.5m) and they can all be considered to have offered good value for money.

While Abramovic was spending hundreds of millions of pounds on established internationals, soon to be followed by the Middle East owners of Manchester City buying even bigger and more expensive stars, Wenger was moulding his team into a sleek and often scintillating football unit that was as easy on the eye as any in Europe. On a par, indeed, with Barcelona.

So how come six seasons have gone by without a trophy? Perhaps Oliver Kay in the Times put it best. "Every Arsenal setback can be put down to an isolated incident – a missed chance, a poor refereeing decision, a defensive error."

Kay was referring specifically to the end of the 2010-2011 campaign but he could have been talking about the whole six years. The point he has highlighted is one that makes Arsenal's "failure" all the more unfathomable and hard to take by those who love the club. Because Arsenal, before the 8-2 aberration at Old Trafford never got walloped. Anyone remember a 5-0 thrashing? Almost always it's that nick or slip or goal-bound drive that shudders the cross bar and doesn't go in. Inches, centimeters, seconds – it's always the one goal that never comes or the split second of genius by an opponent who has never done anything like it before and never will again. Trawl through the results and you will find an incredibly small number of defeats by more than one goal. And, of course, eight draws at the end of this last season defined the whole problem.

But incongruity lurks around every corner as you try to analyse just why it has come to this. Arsenal, the great attacking team, the team that had consistently scored more goals in the Premiership than anyone except Manchester United, the team that, even after they had been knocked out of the Champions League, had still scored more goals in the competition going into the quarter finals than any other team across Europe, had been turned into a team that had become hard to beat. A team that went 16 matches in 2011 without a defeat. A team whose much criticized defence had earned them the points while the forwards, who could not score at home against Manchester City, Sunderland, Blackburn Rovers or, from open play, against Liverpool, had let them down. Even with Van Persie back in the team, mostly fit and scoring away from home so frequently that he created a Premiership record by hitting the net in eight consecutive away matches, they found it difficult to turn one point draws into three point wins.

So it is a little difficult to accept that Arsenal's failure to go on and win any of the four trophies that were still in its sights at the beginning of February – something no other team in the country could claim – was the fault of the defence. In January, Arsenal played no less than nine games – the most ever in one month – and conceded just four goals. Arsenal played Barcelona, the world's greatest attacking machine, twice and, while they had eleven players on the field let in just one goal in 136 minutes play. That's right, this supposedly leaky defence kept out Messi and Villa and their colleagues all but once in 136 minutes and, even after Fabregas' ill-judged back pass let in Messi, were still winning the tie at the Nou Camp until Van Persie was sent off. How bad can a defence be?

Yet when it came down to the crunch, to that fateful week in April when the Premiership was still winnable, six goals were conceded in three vital matches against Liverpool at home and Tottenham and Bolton away. Two of them were penalties and it would have been three had not Wojciech Szczesny saved one from Kevin Davies at the Reebok. (Justice there, because it wasn't a penalty but I will get into refereeing decisions in a moment).

What was more pertinent against Bolton was the fact that Johan Djourou had a bad game. He was due one because the Swiss centre half had been the linchpin of virtually all Arsenal's good defensive performances throughout the season, not least at the Nou Camp when his tackling was brilliant. After making a couple of basic mistakes that almost let Bolton in, he failed to get across the substitute Tamir Cohen in the 90th minute and Cohen's header went over the man on the line and inches inside the near post for the winner. You will read the word 'ironic' frequently in this book and this was a classic example. Arsenal's best defender making the mistake that proved decisive in ending their Premiership hopes by making a very temporary hero of a player whose big 'thank you' was to be released by the club two months later. Football is not a kind, nor a logical, game.

It can also been infuriating. Incredibly, that defeat at Bolton was the first suffered by Arsenal in the Premiership with Djourou in the team since Manchester City scored three times at Eastlands in November 2008. The Swiss defender had missed eight months in between, of course, but in sixteen Premiership starts during this campaign Arsenal had never lost with Johan playing and it was only after he had gone off injured at Newcastle that the team shipped four second half goals to draw 4-4. So the fact that Johan himself was responsible for ending a run of which any defender would be proud was particularly cruel.

And certain sections of the media were not just being cruel but inaccurate when they kept banging on about the frailty of the Arsenal defence and the need for a new goalkeeper and new centre back.

From January 1st to April 2nd 2011 the comparative defensive records of the top four clubs read as follows:

Goals conceded in the Premiership:

Arsenal 7
Chelsea 9
Manchester City 9
Manchester United 12

Now add in this somewhat significant stat: In the eleven matches that are encompassed by the above dates, Arsenal let in just three goals when playing with eleven men. All four of the goals conceded at Newcastle were scored after Diaby had been sent off. The total number of clean sheets kept by this 'leaky' defence in those eleven games? Eight.

A lady called Eleanor wrote on one of the Arsenal Fan websites: "The media just buy into the myth. Their opinions are not based on analysis or observation." It's very difficult to argue with this. It was absolutely amazing to read in late April that Arsenal still needed a goalkeeper. Had they not watched Szczesny? Not seen him make a wonderfully confident Premiership debut at Old Trafford of all places? Had they not seen him make a string of terrific saves, particularly against Spurs and Bolton? Had they not seen a supremely confident 20-year-old come of age, literally and figuratively as the season progressed to stake his claim as Arsenal's number one for the next ten years or for however long Arsenal can cling on to him?

In his first twenty games for the first team, there were two blemishes. One, of course, was the screw up at the end of the Carling Cup final against Birmingham City and that was 75% Koscielny's fault. If you stick a foot in front of your keeper as he is about to gather the ball, what do you expect him to do? He dropped it and Martins scored to give Birmingham victory. The other came against Spurs when Arsenal were leading 3-2. He raced out to try and rob Aaron Lennon and was a fraction of a second late. Some commentators suggested he was a little unlucky because Lennon had pushed the ball too far forward and was not in control of it. But you heard no complaints from this impressive young Pole.

"I was late," he said. "The ref made a good decision."

With that attitude and all the talent he brings to the team Arsenal have absolutely no need to look for another number one goalkeeper.

A centre back? You can always do with another top class centre back. But again, reading all the criticisms about the defence, I saw very little reference to the season-long absence of Thomas Vermaelen until he re-appeared in May. The tall, commanding Belgian had joined at the start of the previous season and, quite apart from impressing with his defensive qualities, he shocked everyone by scoring five goals in his first ten games for the club. There is no point in contemplating how good the defence might have been had

Vermaelen and Djourou played the majority of games at centre back because, as Wenger says, it is no use worrying about players who can't play.

In the meantime, Laurent Koscielny was a bit overwhelmed while making his debut at Anfield and got sent off late in the game against Liverpool for a second yellow. A couple more quirky mistakes before Christmas suggested that the poker-faced Frenchman was an accident waiting to happen. But it was soon evident that he possessed considerable footballing ability and a large number of perceptive fans think he has a future at the club. It should be noted, too, that he only missed one game during that eleven match run in the Premiership which showed the Arsenal defence to be as watertight as any top defence can hope to be.

Sebastien Squillaci arrived from Seville at the start of the season in answer to all the demands for another centre back. Even before Thomas Vermaelen got injured it was obvious Wenger needed more cover in that position and Squillaci was well known to him, having played for Monaco before heading to Spain. It appeared to be a deal done at the last minute and by the beginning of October the Frenchman must have been saying "Zut alors!" or something similar when he woke up in the mornings. He had not only scored a goal for Arsenal in the Champions League at FK Partizan in Belgrade on September 28th but, five days later, was running onto the pitch at Stamford Bridge wearing the captain's armband. Fabregas was suffering from the first of his injured spells and the club's vice-captain, Robin van Persie had played just one game up to that date and was not to be seen again until the return match against Chelsea on December 27th.

Manuel Almunia had captained the team in the previous match but he was now replaced by Lukasz Fabianski and, from the team Wenger selected, Squillaci was by far the most experienced. The choice became a little clearer when, later in the season, Jens Lehmann was asked in an interview in the Arsenal programme who he thought, of the current squad, would go on to make the best manager. "Probably Sebastien," he replied. "He understands the game so well."

So, despite what the manager said after the Bolton defeat, I fail to see how the defensive problems are quite as stark or as gross as the critics make out. Set pieces obviously pose the greatest problem and the figures bear that out – 53% of goals conceded came from set pieces.

And the old cry about the need to sign a good old fashioned English centre half doesn't hold water when you look around at the candidates because, clearly, the best one is not English at all but Norwegian. Brede Hangeland was mentioned last summer as a possible target for Arsenal but Fulham wouldn't let him go. This rock-like figure would be an addition to any team. Last season he made 424 clearances, more than anyone except Blackpool's Ian Evatt who made 430. But English? Paul Merson, who I loved as a player but love a little less as a pundit, sat there in the Sky studio after the Bolton game and came up with the obvious name of Gary Cahill. The Bolton defender is good but no Arsenal centre back had been involved in a 5-0 drubbing as Bolton had been in the FA Cup semi-final against Stoke City just a week before. And three days later Cahill was part of the Bolton defence that let in three against Fulham at Craven Cottage. One of the goals happened because he lost his marker. Cahill's a fine, strong player but suggesting he was the answer to Arsenal's defensive problems was somewhat far-fetched. It was hardly the moment to press his claims.

Having spent fifty years in the business of sports writing, mostly filling the need to meet a deadline with several hundred coherent and properly written words, I am all too well aware of the necessity of coming up with decisive answers to the questions that are raised in the wake of big sporting events. Wishy-washy won't work. You have a sports editor barking at you and a sub-editor screaming for copy and you have to decide, based on whatever incomplete evidence is available to you at the time while you try to make sense of your notes, just what the hell it was that made one team collapse from 2-0 up.

The problem with trying to achieve this while analyzing Arsenal is that no statement the critics can make about them being shot shy; leaking at the back; lacking leadership or whatever is immune from contradiction. Annoyingly, facts keep getting in the way. Paul Doyle in the Guardian came up with a wonderfully comprehensive list of statistics that looked at the 2010-2011 season from a purely factual stand point and, after reading it, one wondered how Arsenal hadn't won the Premiership outright. Look at these figures:

Highest average possession by any team: Arsenal 60%
Most completed passes: Arsenal 444; Chelsea 423
Highest percentage of short passes completed: Arsenal
 92.3%, Man City 90.3
Best shooting accuracy: Arsenal 47.5%
Player with best shooting accuracy: Nasri 65.4%
Best scoring average v minutes on pitch: Van Persie every
 98.2 mins; Berbatov 110.5

Unhappily there was another stat that hit at the root of Arsenal's problems – that stat about conceding goals from set pieces. Arsenal were top of this list with 53%. It was different in the days of Sol Campbell and, more recently, with Kolo Toure in the defence. In 2008-2009 Toure made 129 headed clearances and Arsenal let in almost half as few goals from set pieces – 12 to 23. Maybe Kolo's departure to Manchester City was a bigger blow than was realised at the time.

However, revealing though these stats are, they do not quite tell the whole story. So let's trawl through a few of these attempts at pinpointing exactly what it is that ails Arsenal.

Failure to score at home: The team looks guilty here after losing 0-1 to Newcastle and drawing 0-0 to Manchester City, Sunderland and Blackburn. If a goal could have saved a point against Newcastle (Walcott hit the bar) and one goal each against the other three could have produced three points instead of one, the difference would have been seven points. Fast forward to May Day and Arsenal would have gone into their match against Manchester United just two points behind. Their subsequent 1-0 win would have put them top. So it's the inability to score goals that is to blame! Sounds reasonable – except........Arsenal scored more goals in the Premiership than any other team except Man U and more goals in the Champions League in Europe right up to the quarter final stage, by which time they had been knocked out.

OK, so it is the defence. Letting in an extra time goal at Sunderland to draw 1-1; three at home to West Brom to lose 2-3; four at Newcastle to draw 4-4 after leading 4-0; three at home to Tottenham from 2-0 up; three at White Hart Lane from 3-1 up and two against Bolton at the Reebok to lose 2-1 in the 90th minute – take away one goal from the opposition in all these matches, turning draws into wins or losses into draws and that's an extra nine points. After beating Man U, the title really would have been there for the taking. And yet.............there was that run in January through to the beginning of April when Arsenal had the meanest defence in the Premiership and was producing some herculean stuff against Barcelona. The defence didn't look too bad then, did it? And all without Thomas Vermaelen and, occasionally, Johan Djourou.

So, it's lack of leadership. It's possible we might be getting a little closer to a definitive answer here. That's not supposed to be a criticism of Cesc Fabregas. Despite a very disappointing season, I believe he was committed to Arsenal, at least in the short term, and retains a burning desire to win every time he walks onto the pitch, be it at Arsenal or Barcelona. And, because of his talent and history of achievement, he expects to lead by example. The problem through most of the 2010-11 season was his form which dipped in accordance with his level of fitness. So, much of the time, he couldn't lead by example and his personal frustration – highlighted at the Nou Camp against Barcelona, a match, in hindsight, he should never have played – might have seeped into the team's psyche.

It is no use asking someone to be something they are not and Fabregas, for all his genius, does not have the commanding physical stature of Patrick Vieira nor the sergeant-major personality of Tony Adams. There were times during the season when Arsenal could have done with either or both and, again with the benefit of hindsight, one wonders whether it might not have been a good move to get Vieira back at the club. Not necessarily as captain but just to be around the practice ground and the locker room so as to allow the younger players of this still young team to absorb his winning aura and mentality. Vieira proved that he was still good enough to put in some useful shifts for Manchester City as the season wore on and one wonders what effect he might have had coming on as 75th minute sub, say, against Bolton Wanderers at the Reebok. Jens Lehmann seemed to have a pretty good effect on the club when he returned so surprisingly to assist in the goalkeeping crisis and Szczesny was full of praise for the advice he had to offer. Vieira could hardly have been any less inspirational.

Looking back over these past six years, Vieira is one of the players who might have left too early. He had become a commanding Arsenal captain and it was his leadership qualities that were missed as much as anything.

Mathieu Flamini and Alexander Hleb certainly left too soon for their own good and probably the club's as well. Possibly, as things turned out, so did Gilberto. They all left for slightly different reasons but agents – or, in Flamini's case, family members guiding him – egged them on with promises of greater riches.

It is arguable whether Thierry Henry should have gone just when he did. A dynamic seemed to have developed within the squad whereby he towered over everyone to an extent that was becoming unhealthy. His feats had been so prodigious and his personality so dominating that others were beginning to shrink in his shadow. I have no cast-iron evidence that this was so but the grape vine kept on insisting on it. If anyone was irreplaceable it was this gorgeously gifted footballer – for my money the most thrilling and watchable ever to pull on an Arsenal shirt – and obviously the club suffered from his departure to Barcelona.

None of these players enhanced their reputations at their new clubs. Vieira did all right at Juventus and then Inter but, possibly due to the more technical style of Italian football, he never looked like the dynamic, controlling mid-field force he had been at Highbury.

Flamini took time to settle at AC Milan and never seemed to be sure of his place in the team. But he was certainly missed at Arsenal the season after he left. I remember one particular instance, during the humiliating home defeat to newly promoted Hull City, when Geovanni joined the long list of players who fancied taking long range pot shots at the Gunner's goal and scored with a scorching 35-yarder. My instant reaction was to bemoan the absence of Flamini whose terrier-like attention to his mid-field duties would surely have closed down the Brazilian before he could lift a boot.

Hleb did not take long to discover he had made the wrong move. In less than a year, Barcelona had shipped him back to Stuttgart, where Arsenal had found him, and then his craving for a return to the Premiership led him to Birmingham City. I suppose he got some satisfaction from being on the Carling Cup winning team but he has said publicly often enough that leaving Arsenal has been disastrous for his career.

Gilberto appears to have survived in Turkey, probably because this amiable man is a technically sound footballer with a charming personality. He was well received on his return to the Emirates for a friendly and rightly so.

The same, of course, was true of Henry because he has stated again and again that Arsenal is emblazoned on his heart and that he will be a Gunner till the day he dies. He admitted to feeling very strange having to play for Barcelona against "his team" and was fervently hoping that the two clubs would not be drawn against each other. And then, of course, he proved what an incredible personality he has been in the annals of the club by making that fairy-tale return in January 2012 to score the goal with virtually his first touch back in an Arsenal shirt to beat Leeds United in the FA Cup in front of an Emirates crowd that was having the next best thing to a collective orgasm.

Financially, most of these moves made sense for a club in need of looking after its balance sheet. But one wonders whether Wenger regrets having made one or two when he did.

Had they stayed for a season or two longer the history of Arsenal Football Club might have turned out differently. These are the imponderables to weave into the web of improbabilities, missed opportunities and rank bad decisions that cost Arsenal dear during its barren run.

I've picked out a couple of games during the 2010-2011 season to highlight how closely linked are Kipling's twin imposters of Triumph and Disaster but, of course in the high-octane, partisan and often blind world of club football one thing is certain – they can never be treated just the same.

THE WENGER CODE

3

NEWCASTLE'S IMPROBABLE COMEBACK

And so to St James' Park and an afternoon so bizarre, so unlikely, so completely beyond the realms of logic that one was left wondering how the fates could have woven such a tapestry of joy and despair.

It is important to lay out the exact sequence of events because, in time, the bare bones of the score-line will be written off as just another example of Arsenal frittering away a big lead. In reality, a whole sequence of incidents had to take place to enable Newcastle United to recover from a four goal deficit in the first half and so achieve a 4-4 result. It was the domino theory run amok.

Seldom has the phrase 'a match of two halves' been more apt; seldom has a side so comprehensively outplayed been able to recover some modicum of self-respect, let alone grab a point. Seldom has a referee made so many bad decisions in such a short space of time. And never, surely, has one seemingly unimportant injury substitution led to such a damaging catalogue of events.

Because that's where it started – not with Abou Diaby's sending off but with Johan Djourou's injury in the

47th minute. Everything, as we shall see, flowed from that, a domino effect of extraordinary proportions.

But let's start at the beginning. In just 43 seconds Arsenal were one up. Arshavin flicked the ball to Walcott and Theo slid the ball under Steve Harper. Forty three seconds to split a defence that had been impenetrable through ninety minutes at the Emirates. Is there no logic to football?

And it just got better for the Gunners. In a fraction under three minutes, Djourou connected with his head from an Arshavin cross and watched the ball go in off the underside of the bar. It was Johan's first Arsenal goal and his joy was unconfined. After 10 minutes it started to get ridiculous. Walcott was terrorizing Newcastle down the right and it was his cross that Van Persie hammered past Harper.

Where was the Newcastle defence that had played out of its skin to keep a clean sheet at the Emirates in November? The faces looked familiar – in fact it was the same back four of Danny Simpson, Fabricio Coloccini, Mike Williamson and Jose Enrique. Harper for Tim Krul in goal was the only change and it wasn't Harper's fault that goals were flashing past him all over the place. But they were playing like a different team. Great gaping holes opened up as Fabregas controlled midfield and sent his runners off in so many directions that all the Magpies seemed able to do was flap their wings in despair. Diaby hit a volley wide from a scoring position; Walcott had another go; Harper rushed out to save at the feet of Fabregas after a clever flick from Walcott had put him through.

High up in a corner of the magnificent St James' Park Stadium, the red and white contingent of Arsenal supporters were singing deliriously – two thousand voices clearly heard because 49,000 were virtually silent. And they had more to sing about in the 26th minute as Arsenal's smooth, quick fire passing allowed Sagna to hit a pin point cross for Van Persie and the centre-forward's header did the rest. 4-0.

By the time the fourth goal went in, it had become too embarrassing for some of the St James' Park faithful and they left. Big mistake. Huge. There must have been some red faces in a few Newcastle pubs the next day. But when the half time whistle went, they were having to deal with this amazing stat – in three halves at St James' Park Arsenal had scored eight goals and let in none. The Carling Cup win and now this – how much greater dominance could one team have over another? And how improbable could it be that, when the dust had finally settled, Arsenal would have to face the fact that Newcastle, more than any other side, had ruined their Premiership season, statistically as well as psychologically. Five points lost – five points that would have seen them neck and neck with Manchester United at the end of April instead of six points behind.

But all that seemed inconceivable as the teams returned for the second half. To be fair to the Magpies, they began the second half still looking like a side who wanted to try and score a goal. But a couple of attacks were safely dealt with by an Arsenal back four that had looked totally in control until……..until the Arsenal bench started reacting to a sign from Djourou indicating that he had a problem. Something wrong with his knee apparently. No one had seen a bad tackle or anything – just a twinge in the knee and the Swiss centre back was obviously not confident of putting it through more stress. Fabregas put his arm around Johan's shoulder as he trudged off – little knowing that he was watching two points walk off with him.

Sebastien Squillaci was the obvious replacement. By this time, he had played 15 league games since arriving from Seville in the summer and, generally, had acquitted himself well. But now we started the domino effect – one happening determines the fate of another and then another and then another and then another. No, you couldn't script it. What followed was too improbable.

Exactly two minutes after Djourou went off, Squillaci passed to Diaby. It was one of his first touches and, as so often happens when a player is thrown into the fray, the touch was not perfect. He hadn't quite got the feel of the ball and the surface. So the pass to Diaby – not to any of the other nine outfielders but Diaby – was fractionally short. And who was lurking, ever eager to snap onto a mistake? Who else but Joey Barton? The ever-feisty midfielder came in like a train. It was the kind of tackle that required a first touch of the ball. Absolutely required it because had Barton's flying feet caught any part of Diaby the consequences could have been dire for both parties. For a start, Barton would have got away with nothing less than a yellow and it might well have been a red. And if he had caught Diaby's leg or ankle, the willowy Frenchman could have suffered an injury as severe as he had on May Day 2006 when Sunderland's Dan Smith came scything in and broke Abou's ankle so badly he needed three operations and was out for eight months. That kind of injury scars you even more psychologically than physically.

That was the whole point. Diaby had previous. Barton had previous, big time, in all sorts of ways. The fact that Barton did get the ball, thus making it a legitimate tackle, was not the point – certainly not in Diaby's mind. He knew precisely what damage could have been done if Barton had been fractionally late – we are talking split seconds again – and when he saw who the perpetrator was the fuse box exploded in his brain. Had it been another Newcastle player, he might not have reacted in the same way. Had Barton's tackle been on someone other than Diaby, the result, too, would probably have been different. But it was Barton and Diaby and when Abou, with an open palm, angrily put his hand on the knape of Barton's neck and shoved him downwards, that was it. Red card.

The referee could not be faulted over that decision. But he made his first mistake when he allowed Kevin Nolan to come charging up to Diaby and push him in the chest. Diaby, who was in a red mist by then, reacted by pushing Nolan in the back as the Newcastle captain walked away. But that didn't matter because he was going off anyway. What did matter was that Nolan should have received a yellow card. OK, he was reacting. But how many Arsenal players have been penalized for reacting, rather than perpetrating, a crime? Oh, the list is too long to go into here. What matters is that Nolan escaped and that had a profound effect on what followed.

So Arsenal were down to ten men but still 4-0 up. Silly, a nuisance, but not a situation to create panic. The cushion was still very soft and comfy. And after a couple of Newcastle forays into Szczesny's penalty area, the Gunners began stroking the ball around with the kind of assurance that you would expect from a team that knows it is superior and has a four goal lead to prove it. There followed, in fact, a five minute period when Newcastle were scrambling in defence. Arsenal had a corner, Van Persie had a free quick from a promising angle on the right and then, after a Newcastle corner was safely dealt with, Fabregas sent Walcott through with one of his precision passes and it needed a perfectly timed tackle to prevent a fifth Arsenal goal.

Sixty seven minutes gone and still four goals to the good. The crowd were making a little more noise – not difficult after the stunned silence at the end of the first half – but there was still no hint that the home side could dig themselves out of this very deep trench.

Then in the 68th minute the next domino fell – a touch of a leg by an Arsenal defender and Dowd gave a penalty. A little soft but the sort of decision a majority of refs would have made. But it was the aftermath that saw Dowd in his worst light. After Barton cracked the ball past Szczezny, the young Pole picked the ball up and did not release it immediately. By immediately I am talking about two seconds. That was the time it took for Barton to try and grab it from him and a wild-eyed Nolan to come charging up to him, put his arm around the keeper's neck in a stranglehold and shove him to the ground. On the Richter scale of aggression, the act rated an 8 to Diaby's 6. But Dowd's first act was to give Szczesny a yellow for time wasting. Then, presumably on the advice of his assistant, he waved a yellow at Nolan, too. The assistant referee, who later was so keen to give Newcastle their second penalty when Dowd had been unsighted, could hardly have done anything less. He was standing so close to Nolan when he grabbed Szczesny that he stepped forward to try and physically intervene. He put his arms out as if to start pulling Nolan off the goalkeeper although that wasn't necessary because, realising what he had done, the Newcastle captain released Szczesny quickly.

It must be said the Arsenal players were surrounding Dowd by then, pointing out the obvious, demanding some equality of justice. But Dowd was deaf to their entreaties. There were two factors in play here. If Nolan had received a yellow for the push on Diaby, this second yellow would have had him off. But if his hands-on attack on Szczesny was as bad, if not worse, than Diaby's on Barton, why wasn't it a red? Either way, the match should have come down to ten on ten – a completely different ball game with one team still leading 4-1.

But Arsenal had to soldier on a man short and it started to get more difficult. Nolan got the ball in the net only to be ruled off-side. Arsenal got lucky there. Rosicky who had been brought on for Arshavin was certainly playing the Newcastle captain on-side but he was far from the action, in a wide left back position.

But a second Newcastle goal was not long in coming and there was no argument about this one. Enrique put in a good cross from the left, Leon Best, who had hit a hat-trick against West Ham a week earlier, rose higher than Clichy to touch the ball with his forehead. The ball fell at his feet and he was quick enough to pierce a forest of outstretched Arsenal legs. That goal was clocked at 74 minutes. Now the crowd were stirring and St James' Park was becoming recognizable again, a cauldron of Geordie passion as one of the world's greatest sets of supporters decided that, just possibly, all was not lost. Their team heard the rising crescendo of support and responded.

But they needed some more help from Mr Dowd, or at least his assistant linesman. In the 82nd minute Fabregas, just inside his own half near the Newcastle left hand touchline, left a leg trailing on a tackle and gave away a free kick. Eboue, who had just come on for Walcott, kicked the ball away and got a yellow card. Silly. Given the role he was destined to play in this contest, it was Barton, inevitably, who stepped up to take the long range kick which he pumped across the goal in search of Williamson. Right on the goal line, to the left of the Arsenal goal, three players jumped for the ball – Williamson, Koscielny and Rosicky. Everyone had their arms in their air. The Newcastle defender was not sandwiched but he twisted as he jumped and fell away from the Arsenal pair. Dowd appeared unsighted. Not so the linesman who, as Williamson sat on the turf with arms upraised appealing for a penalty immediately granted the fans their fervent wish. Another penalty. You can watch the video a dozen times and still struggle to see where there was real contact. Like the other two, Rosicky's arms were flapping in the air and they may have brushed Williamson's shoulder. May have. Dowd did nothing until he saw his assistant's flag waving. Everyone, including most of the Newcastle players, looked either stunned or surprised, not least the fourth official on the touchline whose expression when dealing with Wenger's inevitable complaint, looked totally bewildered. As well he might.

So up stepped Barton again and rammed his shot straight down the middle. Szczesny had elected to dive to his left but was so quick to react that he stuck a leg up and actually made contact with his shin. Inches and centimeters again. A fractionally firmer touch and it could have flown wide instead of simply helping the ball into the top of the net.

Now the crowd were in a frenzy and on television analyst Stewart Robson was bemoaning the fact that Arsenal were not trying to play behind the opposition as they had done in the first half. "Arsenal are playing too deep," he said. "That's where they are outnumbered. They need to pass forward and get in behind the opposition."

Six more minutes went by until Rosicky, having sent an intended clearance high into the air, backed into Barton – who else? – while trying to retrieve it. And of course Barton went down like a sack of potatoes. The free kick was about thirty yards out on the Newcastle right. As the cross came in a solid line of Arsenal defenders ensured that it was headed away – I think it was Koscielny who actually made contact. The header was a good one. It flew twenty yards over to the left. It was just what was required – with one caveat. The ball landed right at the feet of Cheik Tioti, the muscular midfielder from the Ivory Coast who was standing ten yards outside the Arsenal penalty area. With a quick glance towards the goal, Tioti unleashed a haymaker of a shot that flew inside Szczesny's right hand post swerving late as it went. The goalie, unsighted by two of his colleagues, had no chance.

Naturally the place went mad with Tioti showing every sign of being ready for the straight jacket such was his delirium. And why not? He had never scored for Newcastle before. He had probably never hit a football with quite such ferocious accuracy before. But then he wasn't the first footballer to say that after scoring against Arsenal. Tioti had just joined the long list which we have documented elsewhere.

And so, improbably, incredibly, Newcastle had levelled from 0-4 down. But where was the panic and the collapse and the lack of leadership and the mental frailty and soft underbelly that so many critics, polishing their well-worn clichés, had trotted out? Which particular goal had revealed any of that? The first penalty? A faint touch of leg on leg? Best's goal – a good one created by one defender not jumping quite high enough? The second penalty which wasn't a penalty? And Tiote's goal – a strike which was brilliant and unstoppable and could only have been achieved if that solid, long range defensive header had landed right at his feet? Where was the panic? Of course Newcastle came surging forward with more confidence and cohesion than they had before. For 43 minutes they were playing at home against ten men. But it should have been ten against ten and the second penalty should never have been given. Those are unarguable facts. And there is no question Arsenal owed a lot to their young keeper because Szczesny made three brilliant saves, once from Williamson header and once diving bravely at the feet of the onrushing Nile Ranger.

But even then it was not over because Arsenal re-discovered themselves tactically in the closing minutes and nearly scored again. Sorry, I'll correct that. They did score again. In the 93rd minute Van Persie thundered a shot into Krul's top left hand corner but was adjudged off-side. Replays suggested it was nothing of the sort. Van Persie was clearly on-side when the pass was hit, moved forward while it was in the air into a fractionally off-side position and then was on-side again when he collected the ball. Difficult for the assistant referee but still not correct. Still Arsenal came forward, getting in behind the tiring Newcastle defence as they had during that first half mayhem. Wilshere was almost through and had Enrique tugging at his shirt with both hands. Not a red card, of course, just a yellow. Van Persie was put through again but this time it really was off-side. Alan Pardew, Newcastle's new manager, was going through euphoria and agony at the same time on the touch line along with every Newcastle supporter. To lose now would have been terrible for them; to win, nirvana. But after 95 mins and ten seconds Dowd blew his whistle for the last time.

4

BOLTON AT THE REEBOK

Of all the frustrations of the previous six weeks this, perhaps, was the most disappointing. Once again the margins were fractional and the refereeing decisions hideous but if a team has three corners against you and scores twice you have nowhere to hide.

As I have said earlier, it was a bitter irony – to pile on top of all the others – that it was Johan Djourou who failed to climb above Tamir Cohen, the new, fresh substitute and prevent the powerful midfielder from heading into the top left hand corner of the net in the 90th minute. Weary legs? Lack of concentration after matches against Liverpool and Spurs in the previous seven days? A bit of both, probably, but an undeserved stain on a wonderful season for this intelligent young man who had shrugged off eight months on the sidelines to step forward as the savior of Arsenal's defence time and again through the season. Had he not been injured at Newcastle; had Sagna not run into him and dislocated his shoulder in a later match, who knows? What if, what if. Endless speculation leads nowhere.

But everyone knew what was required before kick-off at the Reebok. It was Easter Sunday and an incongruously

45

hot sun was blazing down and Arsenal had no illusions about what their egg needed to hatch – a win. The first half performance at White Hart Lane had been so promising with Fabregas looking like the real Fab again and everyone responding at full tilt to his clever prompts, that there was real optimism in the air amongst the loyal throng of travelling supporters. And why not? Bolton might have proved a hard nut to crack a few years back but they had been comprehensively undone 4-1 at the Emirates back in September and they had been thrashed 5-0 by Stoke City of all teams in the FA Cup semi-final at Wembley the previous Sunday. Obviously there was the danger of a backlash from Owen Coyle's humiliated side but there was little sign of it in the opening minutes when Walcott immediately got himself behind the Bolton defence and started causing panic.

And after six minutes Arsenal should have had the opportunity to go 1-0 up. Steinsson wrapped his foot around Walcott's inside the box. If the referee didn't have a perfect view then his assistant had to because it was on his side of the pitch. The commentators were adamant; in the Sky studio Paul Merson and the former Bolton manager Sam Allardyce were adamant – penalty. Not given. The psychological effect of Bolton going 1-0 down after 6 minutes would have been huge considering what they had suffered at Wembley. It would have been a game changer. Just as it would have been against Sunderland at the Emirates. What is the problem with referees and lines people who cannot see what happens before their eyes? Are Arsenal's forwards too quick and clever for them as well as the opposition?

So Arsenal battled on but Bolton, riding their luck, quickly got themselves into the match, mainly through the energy of their captain Kevin Davies, who, dropping deeper, was all over the pitch, defending, probing, running and generally making a huge nuisance of himself. He was aided and abetted throughout by Daniel Sturridge, a loanee from

Chelsea who must have been watching Fernando Torres' embarrassing attempts to open his account for the Blues with a mixture of surprise, resentment and frustration. Because Sturridge had been banging them in for Bolton ever since moving North and up he popped again in the 36th minute to score a goal you don't see too often.

Szczesny had just thrown himself at Lee's feet to hide the embarrassment of the centre backs who had let the South Korean through and then Arsenal conceded a corner. Cahill was up for it and beat Clichy to the header – not an equal challenge really. The header hit Nasri in the stomach and some people thought it had crossed the line as Samir involuntarily edged backwards. That proved to be untrue but it didn't matter because, as the ball bounced back off Nasri's midriff, Sturridge was perfectly placed to lean forward and nod the ball into the net before Szczesny had time to stick out an arm. Sturridge was simply too close.

It was a blow but not irretrievable as Fabregas demonstrated in the 43rd minute when he unleashed a great drive from the edge of the box and then watched the ball cannon off Jaaskelainen's right hand post. The goalkeeper was on his knees ball watching. Once again, it was a matter of three inches between Arsenal and a goal. How often can a team get that close and not score? Twenty one times, according to the stats. That was the 21st time Arsenal had hit the woodwork during the season – more than any other Premiership team. Don't let's get greedy; let's just ask for 25% of those chances to have gone in. Five more goals – what would that have done for Arsenal's season? I know, it's more 'what ifs'. But, more importantly, what does it mean – that Arsenal's attackers are not good enough because they miss by three or four inches? Twenty one times?

It would be difficult to suggest Van Persie was not good enough because, when he scored with a perfect strike in the second half, it was, amazingly, his 18th goal in 19 games in 2011. But, less than twenty minutes later, he got himself into another perfect shooting position, fifteen yards out to the left of the Bolton goal and dragged his shot way wide of the far post. Prior to that, in the final minute of the first half, he had sent a free kick from an inviting position sailing miles over the bar. It must be a very difficult art, this business of kicking a football, because some of the finest exponents make a terrible hash of it quite frequently. Kicking a dead ball with his left foot appears to be something that the Dutchman could do from birth. And he had shown why with his perfectly struck and perfectly placed penalty against Liverpool a week before. But free kicks are obviously different. Trying to get the ball up and over demands a more complicated technique. But Van Persie had mastered it time and again with some wonderful strikes, some saved, some not, in previous campaigns. But not this season. This season Robin had just missed and missed. Perplexing.

Just as perplexing as the decision to give Bolton a penalty within a minute of the re-start. Djourou got close to his man as Sturridge surged into the penalty box and his hand made contact with the forward's arm. Crash, over he went like a felled tree and immediately appealed for a foul. The referee gave it. The decision was as wrong as his refusal to give Arsenal a penalty in the sixth minute. This isn't blind prejudice on my part. Just check the video. So up stepped the Bolton captain to put his team 2-0 up and so push Arsenal's title hopes to the brink. But, by Kevin Davies' standards it was a poor penalty and Szczesny, keeping his eye on the ball as he dived the right way, pulled off a fine save.

Arsenal's response did not bespeak of a team who had lost faith in themselves. Going straight back onto the offensive they finally found the right key and unlocked the door. Van Persie collected a pass out on the right wing, swerved inside, passed to Fabregas who was on the edge of the area with his back to goal and promptly received the skipper's tap back. One touch from VP and Jaaskelainen was diving to his left, hopelessly beaten as the shot curled into the net. Brilliant. That was the 48th minute and shortly afterwards Walcott put Fabregas through but his shot was blocked. Showing intent as ever, Wenger had Chamakh on for Song in the 64th minute and almost immediately Van Persie had that chance to score again. He had time, he was in the right position but the ball was ill-directed and flew well wide of the left-hand upright.

But Arsenal were playing the match in Bolton's half, barely giving the Wanderers a chance to wander into their own, and in the 69th minute Nasri had a golden opportunity to put the Gunners ahead. Clear through on goal with only Jaaskelainen to beat, the little Frenchman who had been dancing around defenders with those twinkling feet of his earlier in the season, blazed straight at the goalkeeper. What did he think? That the bulky Jaaskelainen was made of papier mache? By his standards, Nasri had time to chip, to go round him, to bamboozle Jaaskelainen in all the ways of which Samir is capable. But, by the look of it, he panicked. Obviously he had lost confidence. Why? Because of all the team's missed opportunities of the preceding weeks or because of something he was feeling in his own game? No one was able to ask him that question and it would have been no consolation to remind him that he wasn't alone. But comparing notes with Thierry Henry about the Champions League final against Barcelona would not have been the right therapy.

Chamakh, who had been slotting them away with aplomb during the first three months of the season, was presented with an open goal and missed. Then, in the 74th minute, Arshavin, who had just come on for Walcott, sent Nasri clear on the right. Again, the Frenchman reacted like someone in a hurry, like someone verging on panic as he tried to meet the ball first time and push it back to Van Persie. He could have taken a touch and gone for goal himself. Or he could have taken a touch and crossed it. As it was the ball bounced off his foot and went nowhere.

Still, you felt, the winner had to come. Arsenal were still flowing forward, upping the tempo even as the final minutes drew near and, with eight left, a typically beautiful passing movement flowed across the Reebok's grass and out to Clichy on the left. Runners were in place but the full back's cross was woeful and another chance had gone.

With a few minutes left, Coyle sent on Tamir Cohen, a well-built midfielder who had featured quite often the previous season but had barely started a game for Bolton during the current campaign. His season had been tragically interrupted by the death of his father, Ari Cohen, in a car accident in January. Now he was destined to honour his father in a very appropriate way, albeit a painful one for Arsenal.

But, first, Kevin Davies was finally booked for a bad tackle. As I said he had been his team's inspiration in the first half but that had included a very bad challenge on Song, sliding in from the side and taking the Arsenal man's legs away. The ref spoke to Davies but there was no yellow card for a tackle that certainly deserved one. That was in the 7th minute, less than two minutes after he had booked Muamba for a bad tackle on Wilshire. It was early in the game to book anyone, especially a home player and one wonders whether Mr Jones shied away from booking another Bolton player so soon afterwards, especially the captain. What goes on in a referee's mind? You never know and much of it is probably subconscious. So, ostensibly, Davies' eventual booking should have been a second yellow and therefore a red. But it came in the 88th minute and we are clutching at straws here.

What mattered was the lapse that allowed Elmander to burst through and force another fine save out of Szczesny. All the goalie could do was push the fierce shot away for a corner and, from that, disaster struck. Djourou failed to block Cohen and allowed the Bolton man to lunge in front of him as both went up for the ball in front of the near post. Somehow, with a twist of the neck, Cohen managed to smack a terrific header into the top of the net straight over the Arsenal defender guarding the line. Would it help if Cohen was known as an expert goal scorer with his head from inside the box? Probably not. But, in fact, Tamir was joining the long list of one-off wonders who might never do anything quite as pertinent and spectacular again – a talent Arsenal's opponents seem to have in abundance. It was Cohen's first goal of the season. Of course.

It was also scored in the 90th minute so there was too little time to mount a coherent reply. Wembley all over again.

Putting aside the fact that Arsenal headed home knowing that all their dreams for the season had disappeared, there were two very heartwarming aspects to this match. The first was Cohen's reaction to his goal. He stripped his shirt off to reveal a T-shirt bearing a picture of his late father and was then surrounded by team-mates as he cried on their shoulder. Absurdly, the referee saw fit to stick with FIFA's draconian rules and booked him. Heartless sod is a phrase that comes to mind but I suppose he was just doing his job.

The other was the reception Jack Wilshere received from the fans for whom he had played during his successful loan at the Reebok the previous season. He had been a very popular young man at Bolton, by all accounts, and that was amply demonstrated by the way the Wanderers players reacted to his handshakes and hugs at the end of the match.

On a more frustrating note, it quickly became clear that just about all Bolton had left to offer for this 2010-11 season had been put into gaining this win against the Gunners. Three days later they went down to Fulham and got beaten 3-0 and then, the following weekend lost 1-0 at Blackburn. So, add in the FA Cup semi-final and we have a run of four games in which Coyle's team had let in 10 goals and scored two. But the two were enough to beat by far the best side they met out of that quartet – with due respect to Stoke City, Fulham and Blackburn Rovers. Obviously they had a point to prove in front of their own fans against Arsenal but, really, is logic supposed to play any part in football? Apparently not.

5

A CONFUSING FINISH TO 2010-2011

If there seemed to be little logic that could be attached to Bolton's run of results at the end of the season, try this – Arsenal beat Manchester United and then lost to Stoke City and Aston Villa and drew at Fulham.

In doing so, they dropped out of third position and left themselves with work to do in the qualifying rounds of the Champions League the following season.

In the official website report after the draw at Fulham, Richard Clarke suggested that the team needed the season to have ended a few games earlier. "Now they have the summer to re-build," he wrote. The problem was 90% of the summer had gone before any re-building took place.

Injuries, of course, played their part in the poor performances that followed an excellent one against mighty United but, although they could not be used as an excuse, irony crept in again. Fabregas and Nasri were the players who missed most of those final games and, for Fabregas there would not be any more in an Arsenal shirt. The captain, in fact, missed the victory against Man United, being replaced by Aaron Ramsey who made only his second start since returning from that terrible ankle fracture.

Ramsey celebrated by scoring the winning goal, a coolly taken strike from Van Persie's cut back. United had their chances but, overall, Arsenal were the better side and could look to an unlikely source for their ability to withstand the inevitable raids launched by Ferguson's team in the second half. Coming on at half time, Andrey Arshavin produced one of his best performances of the season. Not through his attacking prowess, although he was active up front as well, but because of how often he tracked back to help out the defence. Some of you who were not there might like to read that sentence again but it was true. Call the little Russian moody if you like but there were moments when he put in some impressive shifts and this was one of them.

So a team that could not find a way past the likes of West Brom, Newcastle and, in a matter of days, Aston Villa, on their own turf now added Manchester United to the two other victories at the Emirates that should have made them world beaters – Barcelona and Chelsea. Did Arsenal need excellence in front of them to produce their own excellence? Were the squad filled with 'big stage' players who only produced their best when inspired by a big occasion? There was plenty of evidence which suggested as much but several instances which refuted it, too. Always a double-sided coin.

For whatever reason, Arsenal went to The Britannia Stadium, one of their least favourite places, and put in a lackluster performance against Stoke City, losing 3-1. Van Persie's 81st minute strike for his 20th goal of the season gave them hope with the score narrowed to 1-2 but within a minute Walters had added a third for the Potters for whom the former Arsenal winger Jermaine Pennant had been prominent throughout.

If that was disappointing, losing at home to Aston Villa was worse. Two goals from the predatory Darren Bent – the first a brilliantly improvised flick – in the first half had put Arsenal on the back foot after the referee had denied them a penalty by ignoring Richard Dunne's fierce tackle on

Ramsey inside the box. It was one of those 50-50 calls but Arsenal weren't getting them.

After a tackle on Bendtner near goal, Van Persie pounced on the loose ball in the 89th minute to prod in a left footed shot but it was too late. The defeat virtually ended the club's chances of finishing third and it was hardly surprising that many fans did not stay to acclaim the squad as they lapped the stadium to say farewell to a season that had been in danger of sending many die-hard supporters to the funny farm.

A visit to Craven Cottage brought down the curtain on this perplexing season and only a goal from Walcott, again scored in the 89th minute after Zoltan Gera had been red carded, prevented it ending on a truly sour note. Theo's effort brought the score back to 2-2 after Zamora's well taken header had put Fulham in front in the 56th minute. Prior to that, another Arsenal old boy Steve Sidwell had scored in the 26th minute before Van Persie equalized three minutes later with his 9th goal in consecutive away matches, easily a Premiership record.

The problem was, of course, that Van Persie had returned from injury too late and none of his amazing goal-scoring consistency was sufficient to gain the points needed to challenge Man United.

Wenger inevitably faced a barrage of questions at the final press conference and made an ill-judged attempt to defend his team by saying they were the only side in the world to have beaten both Champions League finalists, Manchester United and Barcelona, that season.

As one wag put it on the website Just Arsenal, that was like saying Arsenal were the only team in North London beginning with 'A'. What he meant was that as Valencia were the only other team in the world to have played both the finalists that season it was hardly a great achievement. The point Wenger was making was somewhat different, of course. He was trying to make out that his side had the quality to beat the two best teams in Europe and had done so.

The emails flooding cyber space were not kind to Arsene. "Stop your delusions!" wrote Ismarsenal. "Get out, Wenger!" said Dan. Someone called Tordoo wrote, "Anyone who believes we need minor changes is quite insane! We need a complete overhaul of these idiots."

Bob Hope (no kidding) was just as harsh, if less coherent. "Wenger you are irritating me and other supporters with your crap. Against Barcelona we did not deserve to win it was a fluke that proved that we went to Barcelona and we could not even get a shot on goal!"

With a name like that Bob Hope should at least be funny, even if he can't write straight. But no matter how much punctuation was required, the point was clear. There were an awful lot of frustrated and even furious supporters out there who were tired of excuses. Fair enough. They had suffered like all true supporters do and for the fifth successive season the Wenger Code had not served them well.

It takes a strong man to stick to his principles and some would say a blind one when the evidence is stacking up against him. But there was no single explanation as to quite how Arsenal had missed out on so many fronts during the previous nine months. Yes, injuries played their part as did refereeing decisions and the shooting accuracy that is good enough to hit the woodwork but not good enough to end up in the net. That fact that the bar or post shuddered 21 times suggested that the approach work was not that bad as Arsenal also scored 119 goals during the season. That's a ton of goals but it's like a tennis match – you can win two sets 6-0, 6-0 but it doesn't guarantee you win a best of five set match. Three or four goals in games like those against Newcastle, Sunderland, Blackburn Rovers or Liverpool at home not to mention one more against Barcelona at the Nou Camp and the whole story could have been very different.

Wenger's transfer policy has, of course, been at the heart of his Code which, as the years wore on, became tempered by the need to find money to fund the Emirates while still keeping the club out of serious debt. No one, even some of his close friends, have ever been able to determine exactly how much his refusal to splash the cash was because it simply went against the grain and damaged his vision or whether the Board were putting him in a financial straight jacket. The most probable answer is: both.

But before we take a detailed look at the campaign which began so ignominiously in August 2011, I want to examine the conflicting philosophies that are at the heart of the Arsenal problem and look at precisely how Wenger has acted in the transfer market. And whether, if one listens to opposing voices, a change of tack is required.

THE WENGER CODE

6

WENGER AND TRANSFERS

Buy! Buy! Buy! – oh, we have been hearing the cries for years from those who feel that Arsene Wenger's second name is Scrooge and that he harbours Arsenal's riches as if the money was his own. But then, maybe he does. Wenger lives, breathes and sleeps Arsenal and gives every impression of feeling the responsibility of a worried parent dealing in a world of wayward children who seem to have lost all concept of value.

The big money men who have moved into football in Europe over the past decade have more money than they know what to do with – or in some cases not enough real cash to justify their dreams – and have made a mockery of what a sportsman is worth. For Manchester City to come up with £24 million for Yaya Toure and pay him £200,000 a week has no bearing on reality. And it is reality that Wenger attempts to cling to when he assesses what is good for Arsenal Football Club. However, even before the 8-2 debacle at Old Trafford, he was being pilloried like never before for not trying to go head to head with the oligarchs in the transfer market as the season of 2011-2012 dawned.

Of course it has been frustrating and frequently infuriating to hear him fall back on the "we are a very young side" mantra but it would be very difficult to argue that his vision is not better for Arsenal in the long term than that of Manchester City or Chelsea or Tottenham Hotspur, although that will depend to a large extent on whether UEFA's Financial Fair Play rules which come into effect in 2013 actually work.

Meanwhile, we have to admit that the youngsters he has brought through the junior ranks have been exceptional by any standards – Jack Wilshere, Wojciech Szczesny, and Kieran Gibbs have proved their pedigree while Theo Walcott, Aaron Ramsey and Alex Oxlade-Chamberlain were bought for reasonable sums of money considering their youth and have more than justified the outlay. I think many supporters were disappointed when the popular Henri Lansbury and the promising centre back Kyle Bartley were transferred permanently to Nottingham Forest and Swansea City respectively after returning from loans at West Ham and Glasgow Rangers. But there is more youthful talent in the pipe line. Nico Yennaris, a right back or midfielder born in Leytonstone, is still a teenager but appears to have the big match temperament as does the Frenchman Francis Coquelin, another Academy product who slotted seamlessly into midfield or full back when injuries hit in 2011-2012.

And then there is Emmanuel Frimpong, the Ghanaian-born holding midfielder who formed such a great partnership with Wilshire in pre-season a year ago only to be sidelined for eight months with a knee injury. But he is back now and looking strong. These youngsters, along with Sanchez Watt, Benik Afobe, Ignasi Miquel, Conor Henderson, Thomas Eisfeld and the powerful Chuks Aneke can form the nucleus of a great Arsenal side for years to come and with luck, they will all be committed to Arsenal, if agents don't get in their ear.

If any of these players become established stars, and the odds are good that some will, what a contrast they will make to those mercenaries picked up by Man City or, in some cases, Chelsea. It is easy to shout "Buy!" until you get down to the nitty-gritty of who, exactly, is worth the money. Robinho? City paid £32.5 million for a player who blew hot and mostly cold and soon disappeared to Italy. Hernan Crespo? He scored 25 goals for Chelsea and cost £16.8 million. That works out at £672,000 a goal. Worth it? How can it possibly be worth it – especially as Crespo was so unhappy in London that he split the three years he was under contract to Chelsea by playing for AC Milan on loan for a full season. Yet maybe some would consider that a better deal than paying £8.8 million for a chap called Rolando Bianchi. Bianchi, Bianchi......sorry, but it doesn't ring a bell.

These are one-off examples but the true extent of the transfer madness that has hit the Premiership in recent times can be evaluated by the figures below which I have taken from TransferLeague.com. You can pluck just two from the list to make a case for Wenger's policy over that of the Middle East owned Manchester City. Taking the four seasons up to and including 2010-2011, City's net transfer business showed a deficit of £382.5 million. This means that, even having sold the likes of Robinho and Ireland, they had spent £382.5 million more pounds than they had taken in. Over four years that is a staggering sum. Arsenal, in razor sharp contrast, showed a net profit in their transfer dealings over the same period of £11.3 million. That's a difference in outlay of £393.8 million.

Surely the magnitude of that difference in spending has to be reflected in results on the pitch? Surely that kind of investment should, quite quickly, show Manchester City to be a better team than one that is so frugal that it actually makes money on transfers rather than spending hundreds of millions? Then how come Arsenal beat City 3-0 at Eastlands; drew against them at home and only slid beneath them in the Premiership at the last gasp in the final season of the years we are talking about? There's a little matter of qualifying for the Champions League, too. City started spending big two years ago but they have only just managed to get into the European big time and last season made a mess of it when they could not even get into the knock out stages. But, of course, they won the FA Cup. Good effort but, seriously, is one FA Cup win worth a difference of £393.8 million? Isn't that just a little bit too much to pay for one trophy?

A last minute goal in the last game of the season gave City the right to cock a snook at all their detractors because that goal enabled them to pip Manchester United for the Premiership title. But by then some estimates reckoned the owner Sheikh Mansour had poured one billion pounds into the club since 2008.

The fact is that money does not guarantee a team success, even if Manchester City showed what it could do in 2011-2012. And even buying with a real sense of responsibility like Wenger did when he went shopping for Thomas Vermaelen in Holland, does not guarantee the move will succeed. Vermaelen cost a modest £10 million but the club lost him for an entire season after he had been at the Emirates for just one year. A supposedly small injury turned into a major problem and he was out for almost the entire 2010-11 season. Laurent Koscielny, who cost the same amount, played very well as the season progressed but his mistake almost certainly cost Arsenal the Carling Cup. A ten million pound mistake? Cruel but still cheap if winning a Cup would have cost £393 million.

And no matter how one sympathises with those who want instant success, would spending money on Mark Schwarzer or Shay Given really have been worth it? Not, in hindsight, because Lukasz Fabianski was starting to look like a proper goalkeeper by the time he was injured at the beginning of January and then his absence allowed Szczesny to step in and prove what everyone at Brentford had been saying the previous season when he was on loan at Griffin Park – namely that this was a world class keeper in the making. Szczesny is established now and Arsenal need look no further. Money saved.

It has been well documented that there was a financial need for Wenger to tread cautiously in the transfer market because Arsenal's Board of Directors was carrying the weight of the cost of the Emirates Stadium while Highbury was being developed into flats and sold. With a different manager it would probably have been impossible because they would just not have been able to cope. But Wenger was not simply able to keep his purchases low but, through his innate ability to spot and nurture talent, he became a past master at buying and selling for a profit. In many ways it was the most striking aspect of the Wenger Code.

Nicolas Anelka was the greatest example. Bought from Paris Saint-Germain for £500,000, Wenger got a lot of goals out of this major, if insecure, talent and sold him to Real Madrid for a whopping £22.5 million profit. Patrick Vieira was an even better deal if one prioritizes what he brought to the club. After becoming an inspirational captain and banging in that Cup winning penalty against Man U, Vieira was sold to Juventus for £13.7m, having cost £3.5m. Arsenal got plenty of good service out of that flying winger Marc Overmars, too, and, having been bought for £7 million he went to Barcelona for £25 million. Even Thierry Henry made a profit for the club after knocking in a little matter of 226 goals in 367 appearances. Bought for £10.5m, he left for Barcelona for £16m. Talk about value for money!

Profits were also made on home grown players who left the club for a variety of reasons like Ashley Cole who went to Chelsea for £5 million and David Bentley who was sold to Blackburn Rovers for £10 million plus a reported 50% sell-on clause that would bring an additional £7million when he moved to Tottenham. Somehow, Wenger even managed to make a tiny profit on the difficult, self-centred Lassana Diarra who arrived from Chelsea for under £4m (a price that gives you an idea of how pleased they were to get rid of him even though he was nearing the end of his contract) and then moved on pretty quickly to Portsmouth for £5.5m once Wenger decided he was no kind of team player. And then again, there was more money when the Frenchman moved on to Real Madrid. Diarra only played 13 games for Arsenal and I sort of got the drift when I attended a midweek match at Reading when the muscular midfielder had come on as a second half substitute and performed brilliantly. Afterwards, at the press conference, I asked Wenger if he had been impressed with Diarra's talent. "All my players are talented," came the curt reply. Right, I thought, Monsieur Diarra may be French and all that but he's not going to be with Arsenal too long. Of course, he ended up at Real Madrid and struggled to make his mark there, too, although Mourinho refused to let him leave when he arrived to manage at the Bernebeu. Pity that the young man was so impatient. He had the making of a perfect replacement for Vieira.

Although it didn't cost him any money, Wenger would probably rate Diarra as one of his mistakes. There weren't very many of them although I remember reading a hilarious article in the Sun by someone who should have known better. The writer, obviously desperate for an eye-catching angle that day, tried valiantly, if preposterously, to make a case for Wenger being a poor decision maker in the transfer market. The article was based on the two efforts Wenger had made to sign established English talent – the little goal-poacher Francis Jeffers from Everton and the already capped England goalkeeper Richard Wright from

Ipswich. Both found themselves way out of their depth at a club like Arsenal and both moved on – Wright after just one season for £3.5 million having cost six and Jeffers after a slightly longer if just as fruitless stay for £2.5 million, having cost eight.

And then, hurtful though they may be, there are the cases of Fabregas and Nasri. Fabregas arrived from Barcelona as a youth of 16 and went back for £35 million which, as I have mentioned, was cheap at the price. But it threw the spotlight on just how much money Arsenal have taken off Barcelona in recent years. Tot up the total fees paid for Emmanuel Petit (bought from Monaco for £2.5 m and sold for £11m), Overmars, Henry, Hleb and Fabregas, and the total paid by Barcelona to Arsenal comes to just over one hundred million pounds or 128 million euros.

The Nasri deal was not bad either. Wenger paid £12m to Marseille for the Frenchman and collected £25 million from Man City. But if UEFA's Financial Fair Play rules have any bite – which will mean any club exceeding the limit being thrown out of the Champions League – then Sheikh Mansour will just have to zip up his coffers. Between 2013 and 2015 a club will only be able to come up with a net spend of £38 million. If it is really adhered to, the Wenger Code will have triumphed because Arsenal, almost alone amongst Europe's top clubs, will have no trouble because they have never exceeded the limit anyway.

In the meantime, Arsenal fans should try to derive some satisfaction that there has, almost certainly, never been a manager, anywhere in the world, who has made more money for his club through transfer dealings than Arsenal's Scrooge. Generally this delights the Board whose members would obviously rather have a spend-thrift manager than one who throws the club into massive debt.

However, I understand, that there has been the odd occasion when even the Board have wished he might have gone and grabbed a player they liked the look of. Phil Jones was a case in point. The Blackburn Rovers' defender was available in the Christmas transfer window in 2010 and a source tells me there was frustration at the top level when, having been given the green light, Wenger held back and Jones went to Manchester United the following June for £16 million..

But, apparently, there is never any question of the Board telling Wenger what to do in the transfer market. At Board meetings the discussion never goes further than agreeing a sum of money that Wenger could spend on buying players and another, currently set at £120 million, which he can spend on players' wages. "The Board has total trust in Arsene's judgment even if there are differences of opinion," the source says. "Obviously last summer was very difficult because everything was left too late but there was never a question of holding Arsene back. He just felt the best bargains would come at the end of the summer. In the end he got a couple of good ones in Arteta and Santos and maybe even Mertesacker, too. But our manager is his own man. If anyone tried to interfere he'd be off – no question about that."

The actual decisions about which player to buy or sell is left to Wenger and Ivan Gazidis after consultations with the coaches. Once decisions are made it is up to Richard Law to do the dirty work and deal with the agents. Law is an American but he has worked in Europe and South America extensively over the years and is fluent in Spanish and Portuguese. He is perfectly capable of doing the job but, unfairly perhaps, he has had to operate under the shadow of David Dein's expertise in the role. It was much simpler before Dein left in 2007. Friends and neighbours in the North London suburb of Totteridge, David and Arsene would discuss availabilities over dinner and then Dein would go off and work his magic in the market place. Such was his personality and influence that Dein could push Wenger into spending money he might otherwise have been reluctant to spend. And when a player needed to be signed quickly, Dein was always ready to jump on a plane and go get him – like he did with Jose Antonio Reyes during the Christmas break of 2003-2004. There was resistance in his home town of Seville because Reyes had become a local hero but Dein, like some sheriff in the Wild West, flew into town and came out with his man, practically handcuffed to his wrist.

They were viewed as the perfect team, Dein and Wenger, especially when the likes of Vieira, Petit, Henry and Overmars started walking through the door. But when, in the words of the current Arsenal Vice-President, Lady Nina Bracewell-Smith, "David pushed too hard to become chairman and fell out with Danny Fiszman," Dein was ousted from the Board and for a while Wenger was left to try and do the two jobs himself which was hardly ideal for himself or his employers.

When Henri Leconte introduced me to Wenger in the Players Restaurant at Wimbledon in 2008, Wenger said, "I am very disappointed. David leaving the Board is a tragedy for the club."

There are those who will tell you that Dein brought about his own downfall but, as we shall see, a majority of the members of the Arsenal Supporters Trust, no less than 72%, say that they would like to see Dein involved again in Arsenal's affairs.

7

RED AND WHITE

When Peter Hill-Wood, an Old Etonian in manner, accent and upbringing took over the Chairmanship of Arsenal Football Club from his father in 1982, he could hardly have imagined the cast of characters he would find himself dealing with.

It must be said that the five most prominent movers, shakers and shareholders in the club over the past decade make up a very unlikely quintet. And as few have been playing the same instrument – or certainly not for very long – it is hardly surprising that sounds of discord have emanated from the boardroom.

Let's take a look at them. Arsene Wenger, of course stands alone as the man who makes things happen on the pitch. Tall, lean, professorial, a multi-linguist from Alsace who embodies all the romanticism of the French and their love of beautiful things as well as the authoritarian efficiency of his German blood. He wants total control of the team and would leave if he didn't get it.

Then there was Danny Fiszman, the diminutive diamond dealer from Willesden who made his fortune not so far away in Hatton Garden and supervised the move just down the road from Highbury to the magnificent new stadium at Ashburton Grove.

Stan Kroenke, he of the lean and hungry look who might or might not turn out to be dangerous. Silent Stan, as he has been dubbed, shares a German heritage with Wenger but is deeply embedded in the mores and values of the American mid-west and all the very American sporting teams he owns.

If Kroenke also owns Arsenal with his 66.83% shareholding at the last count, he could not cut a more contrasting figure with the man who owns the next biggest chunk of shares at 29.72%. His name is Alisher Usmanov, a great Russian bear of a man who actually hails from Uzbekistan, having been born at a place called Chust in September 1953. He makes Kroenke look almost poverty stricken with reported riches of $18.1 billion. Poor Stan can only scratch together $3.2 billion. Not that the disparity helps Usmanov achieve his ambition of getting a seat on the Board. Kroenke is the fox in the chicken coup and Usmanov the bear beating on the door, never – apparently – to be allowed in.

And then we come to the fifth member of the quintet - David Dein. He is, without question, the catalyst for the simple reason that, without him, none of the four people mentioned above would have got a foot in the door at Arsenal.

Dein, who shared a Jewish North London background with Fiszman, made his fortune in trading and importing commodities and, after buying 16.6% of the club shares for £292,000, was elected to the Board in 1982 and was Vice-Chairman from 1983 to 2007. At the time, Hill-Wood was surprised that anyone would want to pay as much for shares in a football club and called it "dead money". He probably hasn't been invited to Dein's yacht which is very much alive in the water in Turkey.

A young, brash go-getter, Dein was pictured in night clubs with Charlie Nicholas, who had just signed from Celtic, and generally acquired a rather racy reputation. But Dein was also putting Arsenal on the fast track to a level of commercial success none of the Board of that era had ever seriously contemplated.

All manner of merchandise, headed by replica shirts with players' names on the back; sponsorships and other money gathering ideas that only Manchester United and, perhaps, Liverpool had been exploring transformed the financial fortunes of the club. He helped create a bond scheme that enabled the complete re-building of both the North Bank and Clock End at Highbury after the Lord Justice Taylor report had demanded all-seater stadiums following the Hillsborough disaster. No doubt urged on by his American wife, Barbara, who is an avid tennis player, Dein also gave his full support to the creation and promotion of Arsenal's women's team which has been winning titles ever since.

Seeking more business expertise, Dein invited Fiszman to join the Board but that was after he had spotted the genius of Wenger during Arsene's time at Monaco and tracked him to Japan where the Frenchman was honing his Code on how to run a football club with Nagoya Grampus 8. "Arsene WHO?" screamed the headlines when Wenger was named as successor to Bruce Rioch in September 1996. We soon discovered who Arsene was.

With his worldwide contacts, partially as a result of his work with UEFA and FIFA, Dein met Kroenke who showed interest in expanding his growing empire of US sports franchises overseas. Dein introduced him to the Board and, initially, Hill-Wood was appalled. In a voice that harkened back to the long lost days of the Empire, the chairman uttered the famous phrase. "He's not our sort."

But he soon was. On further examination it became clear that Kroenke was a very formidable and well respected owner of the Denver Nuggets basketball team; the Colorado Rapids, a soccer team of the MLS which had already forged a relationship with Arsenal; Colorado Avalanche of the National Hockey League and the St Louis Rams of the NFL. It was an impressive list.

When Dein's ideas to build at a site near King's Cross or share Wembley Stadium as the club searched for a larger ground were pushed aside by Fiszman's bigger vision, the pair's relationship started to fall apart. Sadly, it was Danny, who was to die of cancer on 13th April 2011, who led the move to have Dein ousted from the Board. "David was pushing too hard to become chairman and started threatening people," Lady Nina Bracewell Smith, who was also asked to leave the Board, told me. "It was a terrible shame. We were allies but he just saw things differently to other members of the Board. I had no desire for him to leave the club. David has done more for football than most people and has contributed tremendously to Arsenal's growth. But a lot has happened since he left. It would be difficult to re-create the magic."

That, however, does not mean Dein doesn't want to try. He is, as he jokes with friends and supporters who come up to him every match day at the Emirates, putting himself "on the bench" hoping that an opportunity arises. At the moment, it is not apparent how that can happen.

Being thrown off the Board of a club he had poured his heart and soul into for 25 years was obviously devastating to David. But, despite making himself rich by selling his shares, he remained loyal to Arsenal. Ken Bates, 'Mr Chelsea' for so many years, ended up at Leeds United; Peter Ridsdale left Leeds and went to Cardiff. Dein does not want to be associated with any other club.

"Red and white are the colour of his heart," said Wenger who asked his friend if he should leave, too, when David was ousted. Dein told him no. "The club needs you," he said.

It was no co-incidence that Red and White should be the name of the organization that Dein joined as Chairman in the summer of 2007, having sold his 9,027 Arsenal shares to Red and White's co-owner, Usmanov, for £75 million.

"I always thought he was a seller," huffed Hill-Wood who had been part of the agreement the Board had made on Dein's departure that there would be a 'lock down' on directors selling their shares for a year. Not long after the lock down was lifted, Hill-Wood became a bit of a seller himself, getting rid of £5.5 million worth of his own shares to Kroenke.

So, initially, Dein tried to see what he could do to get Usmanov onto the Board. But he was re-buffed at every turn. After a year he decided that he might be the stumbling block to progress and resigned as Chairman of Red and White Holdings. It made no difference. Fiszman hadn't liked Usmanov and now Kroenke either didn't like him or saw the Uzbek as a direct threat or both. The door was locked.

"What has surprised us most is that Kroenke even refuses to take a meeting with us," says Rollo Head, the company's PR spokesman. "Neither Alisher or his partner Farhad Moshiri have ever done anything to suggest that they do not have the best interests of the club at heart. We believe there should be investment so that money could be freed up for Arsene Wenger to spend. But we would never tell him how to spend it. Alisher has a wide interest in sports and is President of the FIE (The International Fencing Federation) and was involved with the London Olympics. But he has a reputation for never meddling too deeply in the numerous companies he owns."

And the billionaire does own a lot. Having made his fortune in metals and lumber in Uzbekistan, he now has numerous interests in Russia including being co-owner of 7TV and Muz-TV federal channels in Moscow and 35 regional broadcasting stations. He is also co-owner of MegaFon, Russia's second largest mobile phone company and personally owns a publishing house Sekret Firmy as well as having taken over the newspaper Kommersant. In addition there is Digital Sky Technologies and a majority shareholding in Metalloinvest, a Russian industrial conglomerate.

I thought my friend Ion Tiriac had broad interests in Romania, which he does from a Mercedes franchise to Tiriac Airways, but Usmanov seems to be in a different league. He was rated as the 28th richest man in the world in 2011.

It is, of course, inevitable that some people at Arsenal would view Usmanov warily, even with suspicion. He has, after all, been called a crook on the basis of having been imprisoned for bribery and extortion by the military tribunal who happened to have their hands on power in Uzbekistan in 1980. In those days when it was still a part of the Soviet bloc, corruption was rife in the satellite states and who knows what jealousies arose when bright young men started making money.

The only thing we have to go on is that in July 2000, when something a little more akin to democracy had arrived, Usmanov was cleared of all charges by the Supreme Court of Uzbekistan which stated that the original evidence against him was fabricated.

So now we have the strange situation of a very wealthy man, who seems to be a genuine fan of the club wanting to invest and being held at bay for fear of..........for fear of what? Kroenke has repeatedly said he is in it for the long haul and has no intention of selling his stake so his position would seem impregnable. Would another voice on the Board be so disruptive?

If one takes the opinions of the Arsenal Supporters Trust as some barometer of how the fans think, 82% of those responding to a poll think that Red and White should be offered a place on the Board; 75% are dissatisfied with Kroenke's explanation of his vision for Arsenal Football Club yet, confusingly, 60% approve the idea of a self-sustaining business model which is what the Board stand by. And 77% support Wenger despite 38% being dissatisfied with recent performances on the pitch.

Having studied the various elements and spoken to people on both sides, I must confess to harbouring contradictory opinions myself. I am certainly a supporter of Arsene Wenger, truly believing him to be one of the great football managers of all time, notwithstanding odd moments of irrational behaviour and his reluctance to spend what is available to him. However, I fully applaud his desire to promote youth from within the club and develop a style of play that is a delight to the eye. Many, probably a majority, of Arsenal's supporters would disagree, but I really would prefer to see Arsenal fail narrowly than winning with the brand of football Chelsea have produced in recent seasons. I want to delight in the highest levels of skill footballers can aspire to and we have seen that frequently, if not consistently enough, from Arsenal over the past decade.

In the last chapter I pointed to Wenger's brilliant dealings in the transfer market and the figures have only been improved by the £22 million received from Manchester United for Robin van Persie.

But David Dein, Alisher Usmanov and a fair percentage of supporters want to see Arsenal put out the best team money can buy. The letter Red and White Holdings published as soon as it became clear that Van Persie was at odds with the club's philosophy and wanted to leave contained many valid points even though those loyal to the current regime saw it as an attempt to disrupt the smooth running of the club.

In part the letter read: "You can try and put a good face on a bad game as long as you want, pontificating about the merits of this model but it will not hide the obvious fact that it does not allow our great manager to fully realize his managerial talent and deliver success to the fans who are paying the highest prices in the land."

To ram home the point, the letter went on, "Yet again we are faced with losing our true marquee player because we cannot assure him of a future direction and the confidence we can win trophies."

In as much as Van Persie did seem to be pursuing trophies as opposed to an increased wage package (Arsenal were offering extremely generous terms to re-sign), there is some truth to all that but the critics still thought the letter reflected poor judgment on the part of Usmanov.

Rollo Head, however, insisted that it was valid criticism and that Red and White would never be so critical publicly during the season.

The only reason I lean towards Usmanov over Kroenke is not because of their positions or visions for the club. It is much more basic and emotional than that. As a fan of 60 years standing I am offended by the fact that Arsenal is owned by a man who cannot be bothered to attend more than two games a season and flies home three days before a match against arch-rivals Tottenham Hotspur after attending a Board meeting in London. Obviously watching one of his American teams was more important to him. Fine. But if that's how he feels he shouldn't own Arsenal.

Maybe Usmanov would not be any better or maybe he could be worse. But he appears to be a much more genuine fan who turns up regularly to watch games.

It doesn't really matter if this view is ridiculously naïve because I think we have reached a stalemate and nothing will change unless Arsenal have another season that turns out to be even more frustrating than the last two. And no one who really loves the club wants that to happen.

8

Season 2011-2012

OWN GOALS AT BLACKBURN

You go to Ewood Park on a wet and windy autumn day, score three stunning goals and lose? Really? Scoring two at Old Trafford for the first time in yonks and losing by some absurd score was bad enough but this, in some way, was even more ridiculous. Talk about the improbable again.

Just look at the stats:

Possession: Blackburn 31%, Arsenal 69%
Shots on target: Blackburn 4, Arsenal 9.
Corners: Blackburn 2, Arsenal 13
Passing success: Blackburn 70%, Arsenal 85%.
But, of course, the only statistic that mattered was Blackburn Rovers 4, Arsenal 3.

Not sure how much more of this Arsenal fans can take, let alone poor old Wenger. There has to come a time when a ball fired across the goal does not hit a defender's knee (Song in this case) and bounce into the one corner of the goal that Szczesny couldn't reach – a space of about three feet. There has to come a time when another cross, which Szczesny gets a finger to, doesn't hit a defender's feet (this time it was Koscielny) and bounce straight into the goal. And maybe there will come a time when touch judges don't allow off-side goals against Arsenal (other teams suffer, too, of course). But the man's flag remained resolutely at his side on this occasion as Yakubu scored his second from an off-side position. Close – but still off-side.

So there it was – Arsenal played most of the football (much of it breathtaking stuff in the first half) scored wonderful goals through Gervinho and Arteta (their first for the club in the Premiership) and Chamakh, whose flying header from Van Persie's pinpoint cross brought back memories of the centre-forward he had looked like on joining the club a year before.

But Blackburn replied at 0-1 with a terrific side-footed goal from Yakubu (his first for Rovers after arriving from Everton) the Song own goal from 1-2 down and then Yakubu's off-side effort and Koscielny's own goal to go ahead 4-2. It was lashing down when they scored their goals and driving rain is not Arsenal's favourite weather mode. Remember when the heavens opened to produce the father and mother of all storms over the Stade de France when Arsenal were leading Barcelona 1-0 with ten men in the Champions League final? That was only marginally worse than the downpour at Ewood Park. For Arsenal that old truism that it never rains but it pours rings very true indeed.

So Blackburn won because, as I have mentioned before, it doesn't matter how you play, it's all about getting the ball in the net.

Yet the probability is that, if you score three goals at difficult places like Ewood Park, you tend to get at least a point. But, as we keep finding out, Arsenal, at this particular period of their history, don't deal in probabilities. It's all too improbable.

There were ironies, too. Blackburn's two central defenders, Christopher Samba and Scott Dann could both have been wearing Arsenal colours if rumoured transfer dealings had worked out differently. Samba, in particular, had been mentioned time and time again as an Arsenal target but Rovers were obviously loathe to let their giant, inspirational captain go and, right on deadline, it was Mertesacker who came in.

The irony was undeniable but it was far-fetched to suggest, as some reports did, that Samba would have made the difference. In fact one reporter even went as far as to say Arsenal would have won if Samba had been playing instead of Mertesacker. If the German missed a golden opportunity to draw Arsenal level in the dying minutes with a header that flew three feet over the bar, then Samba had missed an even simpler chance for Blackburn in the first half. And neither he nor Dann could do anything about Arsenal's two brilliantly worked goals early on nor could they stop the leaping Chamakh getting in between them for his header. So they were no more infallible than Arsenal's error-prone rearguard.

The two own goals really had to be seen to be believed. The first came about when the much-criticised Arshavin tracked back and gave away a free kick with a fractionally mistimed tackle just outside the penalty area on the left hand side. Where was the new boy Santos? Not in the picture although it was his position the little Russian was covering.

The cross came in, Samba leapt for it – his vast body obscuring any view of the ball arriving - and it may or may not have flicked off the top of his head. At any rate, it dropped right onto Song's upper knee. Alex had another Arsenal defender between him and the goal as well as a Blackburn attacker who had moved past him by the time the ball made contact with his knee. He pushed his leg slightly forward in an involuntary action and the ball somehow managed to find its way through two players and past Szczesny's outstretched left hand. Fluke doesn't begin to describe it.

The second happened after Sagna had gone off injured and had been replaced by Djourou. Arsenal had fought back well from the shock of going 3-2 down when Yakabu slid in another free kick from that off-side position. After good work from Arshavin and Van Persie, both of whom had shots blocked, they forced a couple of corners. But the breakaway from the second spelt more disaster. The speedy Hoilett broke down the left and, with Santos nowhere in sight, it was Djourou, racing over from the right back position who got in the first challenge. It was a desperate lunge but he seemed to get a fractional touch on the ball. To no avail. It bounced straight on to Hoilett's leg and rolled forward for him to continue his electric run. The Rovers man got to the by-line, nipped past Song, and tried to find a colleague running up behind Koscielny who was well placed, covering the angle behind his goalkeeper. But, in a reversal of the Carling Cup fiasco, Szczesny, with a desperate dive to his right, got a tiny touch and the ball was at the Frenchman's feet in a flash. But Koscielny's feet were not positioned right and, with no time to adjust, he nudged the ball with his right boot into the empty net.

Koscielny is a talented footballer but, as we saw on his debut at Liverpool and, of course, at Wembley, he is accident prone. So was Gael Clichy. There doesn't seem to be an explanation for it. But it's more than a team lacking confidence at the back and trying to bed-in two newcomers can handle.

The captain, not surprisingly, was frustrated beyond measure. "Every time we make a promising start, we just keep making the same mistakes and that is surprising," said Van Persie. "It frustrates me. We were much better than them and even now I can't see how they scored four goals against us."

Wenger was unusually critical. "Our performance today was terrible. At the moment if you look at the number of points we have given away, that's not good enough. You cannot concede four goals as we did today. I believe this group of players will take off but it's important that we get quick results."

Of course, the media started focusing on Wenger himself, suggesting that his job was under threat. But that wasn't the issue. The issue was how to stop leaking goals. At the other end of the pitch, there seemed little to worry about. Gervinho and Arteta had looked capable of scoring and did so and, even without them, Arsenal had scored two good goals against Manchester United. Suddenly the problem had switched from attack – where the problems started midway through last season – to a defence that didn't look secure enough to withstand a perpetual battering of sheer bad luck. Sorry to use that word but if there is such a thing as good luck, Arsenal, at this stage of the season, certainly weren't getting any.

As a new week dawned in mid-September, Arsenal were desperate for a diversion and the third round of the Carling Cup against Shrewsbury Town at the Emirates arrived spot on time. Here was a chance to present some of the new talent Wenger had brought into the club and he seized the opportunity to a greater extent than anyone expected. None of the eleven who started at Ewood Park made the team. Johan Djourou was named captain and two other subs who happened to be international captains, Yossi Benayoun of Israel and Ju-Young Park of South Korea, were brought in to offer experienced support.

But otherwise it was a night for the kids – Carl Jenkinson, Emmanuel Frimpong, Francis Coquelin, Ignasi Miquel with the most touted of the lot, Alex Oxlade-Chamberlain taking Walcott's position on the right wing. From the word go, Chamberlain looked poised, cool and talented. Which is more than you could say for the defence. The fact that Shrewsbury actually took the lead after 15 minutes when their centre forward, James Collins, rose unchallenged to head past Lukasz Fabianski, who might have come for the cross but didn't, was almost the least of it. Just before that, the speedy Marvin Morgan had watched his shot trickle onto the upright with Fabianski gazing at its progress.

After the goal, Morgan had another free shot and missed. There was a deflection from Mark Wright which might have gone in and then a corner which Fabianski missed completely. 3-0 to Shrewsbury would not have been an incorrect score.

Thankfully Arsenal, who had required the Shrewsbury goalkeeper Smith to make two great saves in the first five minutes, regained some measure of control and, with the long legged Jenkinson ever eager to get forward, some quality crosses started to test the Division Two defence and in the 32nd minute, the breach was made. A defender could only flick on an excellent cross from Jenkinson and the ever alert Gibbs found the tiniest space between Smith and his right hand post to head in.

After the interval Arsenal looked more assured and Park started to show what he had to offer with a couple of good runs and a shot that was blocked. But it was the speedy Chamberlain who kept catching the eye and after he, too, had seen an effort blocked, the 18-year-old let fly from 20 yards. The shot carried too much power for Smith who dived too late and the ball flew under his body.

So, after 57 minutes of less than convincing football, Arsenal led 2-1. It stayed that way until the 79th minute when another 18-year-old Oguzhan Ozyakup fed the tireless Benayoun and the Israeli picked his spot for the third goal. By then the Japanese teenager Ryo Miyaichi, who had replaced Park, had shown glimpses of great pace on the left. But Chamberlain had, undoubtedly, been the star of the show and he received a big round of applause when Wenger took him off in the 89th minute to allow the imposing Chuks Aneke a brief taste of first team football.

So pluses and minuses. The teenage attackers had looked full of promise and Jenkinson, too, suggested that he could mature into a really threatening right back once he gets a little more top flight football under his belt. It was amazing to realize that he had played only eight first team matches for Charlton Athletic before being snapped up by Arsenal.

But Jenkinson was also part of a defence that still looked hugely vulnerable. Had Djourou lost a fraction of pace in the summer? He appeared heavier in the thigh than he had the previous season and his first showing as an Arsenal captain was not one he will remember fondly. Sad because like some other Arsenal centre backs before him – Pascal Cygan comes to mind – he is a better footballer than some give him credit for.

But the media pounced once again on the defensive performance and it has certainly given them plenty to chew on. Not surprisingly Wenger found himself under fire with some suggesting his job was on the line. "Not so," said the CEO Ivan Gazidis, coming to his manager's aide.

Gazidis has not been very visible since assuming the duties that used to be done with greater transparency by David Dein before the unfortunate Boardroom coup of 2007 but he stepped forward on this occasion with a speech at a lunch for sports business leaders in London.

First of all, Gazidis assured everyone that the American owner, Stan Kroenke, had been "intimately involved" during the frustrating summer and fully supported both Wenger and the club's "self-sustaining" model. Gazidis also refuted assertions in the media of panic buying at the very end of the transfer window.

"It was not panic buying," Gazidis insisted. "We are not just going to spend money because we are under short term pressure. We have kept our powder dry. Arsene is very strong at keeping discipline and finding where the value is."

Gazidis added that there were funds available to buy more players in the January transfer window or the following summer if Wenger felt it was necessary to strengthen the squad.

The following weeks would determine that. Next up at the Emirates – Bolton Wanderers and Gary Cahill at centre half. More tests and comparisons for Mertesacker and that struggling defence.

9

VICTORY OVER BOLTON – THE TIDE TURNS

Looking back, Arsenal's 3-1 victory over Bolton Wanderers at the Emirates on 24th September 2011 was a lifeline to salvation. Under normal circumstances, it would, of course, have been routine. No matter what disasters had befallen the team at the Reebok in the depths of winter a few seasons before, beating Bolton at home had never posed much of a problem. Five wins out of their previous five meetings in the Premiership offering evidence of that.

But this was different. A draw would have been bad. A defeat catastrophic. Criticism of the team; of Wenger; of the whole structure of the club was reaching a crescendo as Robin van Persie led the team out. But that was in the media and the cascade of critical blogs that were flooding cyber space. In the official programme, the Captain's notes told a slightly different story.

Reflecting on how important the Carling Cup victory over Shrewsbury had been, Van Persie made reference to a dinner the team had enjoyed on the Wednesday night. "We had a really good team dinner," the captain wrote. "Most guys were dancing and everyone really enjoyed it. So all the fans should know that we are happy and united as a squad."

After his own dancing feet had helped secure a resounding 3-0 win, Van Persie referred to the party again in his post-match interview. These things really do matter and there was growing evidence that the team spirit of this particular bunch of players, shorn of Nasri's disruptive egotism and a former captain who was hankering for his homeland, was becoming an important factor in the team's resurgence.

And despite the horrors of Old Trafford and Ewood Park, which had contributed to Arsenal going into the Bolton match placed just above the relegation zone at 17th in the league, there had been other performances to suggest the situation was not quite as dire as some people were insisting.

A home game against newly promoted Swansea had produced a not very convincing 1-0 win and three vital points but, with hindsight, the Welsh team were proving themselves to be one of the best equipped new arrivals from the Championships we had seen in recent years and were never in danger of slipping back. So the victory was more valuable than it looked at the time.

Then came the first foray into Europe proper and a visit to Borussia Dortmund at their huge stadium which offers such tumultuous support. It was never going to be easy. Nevertheless, the much-maligned defence which lined up as Sagna, Mertesacker, Koscielny and Gibbs for this encounter, looked very solid in the face of some fierce German attacks and when Walcott slipped a pass through for Van Persie to run onto and lash home in the 42nd minute, everything seemed under control. And it was until the pot-shot routine worked for the opposition once again.

Gibbs did his job by heading out from a defensive position in the 88th minute but the ball landed smack on the right foot on substitute Ivan Perisic and, just like Tiote at Newcastle and Rose at Tottenham, he swung a leg and the ball arrowed on the volley straight into the back of the

Arsenal net. It was becoming laughable. Something tells me that Perisic is not going to score a goal like that again – ever.

And it could have become an even nastier joke had Szczesny not pulled off a magnificent save from the dangerous Robert Lewandowski in the last minute of regular time. So the possibilities went from three points, to one, to none in the final minutes but in the end the compromise of the single point was well earned and, all things considered, Arsenal's new European campaign had got off to a solid start.

But that could not wipe out the fact that Arsenal, by mid-September, had made their worst start to a domestic league campaign since 1953-54 when they were defending the title Joe Mercer's side had won the previous season. So the Bolton match was huge and nerves were still on edge when half time arrived and the score remained 0-0, due largely, it must be said to a brilliant save from Szczesny who flew to his left to palm away a stab at goal from Darren Pratley.

But, probably to the annoyance of those who had lingered over their lager at one of the Emirates' bars, those nerves were calmed within 35 seconds of the re-start. Ramsey carried the ball forward, passed to Van Persie who rounded Fabrice Muamba and unleashed a powerful left footed drive between Jaaskelainen and the near post.

In the 55th minute Walcott's acceleration towards the edge of the penalty area proved all too much for David Wheater, a large and not particularly dexterous centre half. Wheater looked as if he was desperately trying to avoid bringing the flying winger down but the slightest touch sent Theo sprawling and, with no other defender between Walcott and the goalie, the referee had no option. Wheater was off.

Arsenal were starting to relax by this time; the tempo was picking up and Bolton were chasing the game. Speed was the essence and Walcott had it. Racing down the right, leaving everyone in his wake, this much criticised footballer laid on the most perfect pass for his captain and Van Persie only had to side-foot the ball into the net to claim the 100th goal of his Arsenal career. He was the 17th player in the club's history to reach that landmark and, as he said afterwards, "It made it extra special for me today."

The pass was extra special, too, which was why Robin turned during his celebration and pointed, emphatically, with both arms outstretched at Theo. "I love Theo," he was to say later in the season. No surprise, there. Centre forwards tend to love wingers who give them pin point passes in front of goal and Walcott continued to do that all season.

In fact, Walcott did it thirteen times, quite apart from scoring 11 goals himself and it was this RvP/Walcott double act that, more than anything else, dragged Arsenal from the depths and enabled them to shock the pundits by finishing 3rd in the table by season's end.

But that was still a long way off and what was needed now was just a little varnish to finish off a satisfactory, morale-boosting afternoon. Alex Song provided it, curling in a cool, right foot shot from the edge of the box after receiving Ramsey's pass. The joy on the Wenger's face was a sight to behold.

10

LONGSHOT DEFEAT AT TOTTENHAM

It was back to the Champions League with a home game against Olympiacos on 28th September and the Arsenal faithful – those still full of faith and those searching for other formulas – did not have to wait long for more positive input.

And the fact that it came as early as the 8th minute from the club's most exciting new arrival only made it better. Alex Oxlade-Chamberlain, son of the former England winger Mark Chamberlain, had been bought from Southampton, Walcott's alma mater, for £15 million and he swiftly re-paid some of the debt.

The young man who looks like a footballer of class from his boot laces to his fingertips, needed a touch of luck as he opened the scoring but no one would begrudge him that. Song passed inside from the right, The Ox, as he would inevitably become known, didn't take it cleanly but grabbed the second chance as the ball bounced back to him from Ivan Marcano's shin. A couple of strides to make room for himself and the shot was fired goal-wards, fooling the keeper as it went straight through the legs of the former Aston Villa defender Olof Mellberg.

The Ox celebrated with all the wild delight of an 18-year-old and no wonder. He had just become the youngest English goal scorer in Champions League history.

In the 20th minute it got better. Andre Santos may have shown himself to be a bit of a heart-in-the-mouth defender since arriving from Fenerbahce but he is great going forward and he proved how beneficial it is to have a goal-scoring left back. (Yes, Gael Clichy, I am thinking of you). Rampaging down the left, Santos provided a good cross for Marouane Chamakh. But boots collided as a Greek defender slid in to meet the ball at the very same instant as the Arsenal man reached for it. Unintentionally, the collision provided the perfect pass back to Santos and the Brazilian decided to put an end to this passing stuff and whack it into the net himself. Which he did. 2-0.

The team from Athens were by no means out of it. Their bustling, quick-passing style was examining the defensive qualities of Arsenal's back four which had Song proving his versatility once again by standing in the for injured Koscielny at centre-back. However none of them could prevent David Fuster reducing the lead in the 27th minute when he planted a good header past Szczesny.

The game remained very much in the balance during the second half and Arsenal escaped when Vasilis Torosidis cut inside Santos and rammed a shot against the bar. Van Persie had been left on the bench for this match but, in the 70th minute he and Ramsey were brought on and Arsenal did well to hang on to a precious win, thanks in part to some sterling work in midfield from that young power-house Emmanuel Frimpong and the experienced Mertesacker behind him.

The best thing you could say about September was that it had ended better than it had begun, not least because Wenger was able to celebrate fifteen years at the club on the 30th of that month with an endorsement from faraway owner Stan Kroenke ringing in his ears.

Sir Henry Norris (middle) rescued Arsenal from bankruptcy and oversaw the club's move from Plumstead to Highbury in 1913.

Herbert Chapman, a contender with Arsene Wenger for the title of "Arsenal's Greatest Ever Manager".

Doug Lishman, one of the author's boyhood heroes, in action at Highbury.
Lishman played for Arsenal between 1948 and 1956, scoring 137 goals.

Tough-tackling Joe Mercer played 275 games for Arsenal between 1946 and 1955 winning two League titles and one FA Cup winners' medal.

This restaurant, formerly named La Crois d'Or, was owned by Wenger's parents and is was here that Arsene spent much of his childhood.

FC Duttlenheim - Class of '68. Two of Arsene's former team-mates: goalkeeper, Claude Kocher (left) and left-winger, Joel Muller.

Mr. Arsenal. This statue of Arsenal legend Tony Adams was unveiled at The Emirates Stadium on 9th December 2011 by Arsenal Chairman, Peter Hill-Wood.

Theo Walcott at the Emirates during a Champions League game against FK Partisan. Many Arsenal fans will be hoping that Theo will be committing his long-term future to the club following the departures of Robin van Persie and Alex Song.

Alex Oxlade-Chamberlain. The Ox could be the star of the Arsenal team for many years to come and is already a regular for Roy Hodgson's England side.

Theo Walcott and Alex Oxlade-Chamberlain unwind during Arsenal's tour of the Far East and discover that the club has more fans in China than they thought!

New signing Lukas Podolski in action during a pre-season friendly against FC Cologne. Podolski scored twice in the 4-0 victory and was rewarded with a few recitals of, "He scores when he wants…." by Arsenal fans keen to show the departing Robin van Persie their feelings.

Striker Olivier Giroud became the 24th French player to sign for Arsenal under Arsene Wenger. Supporters will be hoping that he finds the shooting boots that helped him bag 25 goals for Montpellier in 2011-12.

Santi Cazorla's has settled in quickly to life in the Premier League and is rapidly becoming the new favourite of the Arsenal faithful.

We all know what owner's endorsements of managers can mean but this one carried an air of genuine authenticity about it despite the fact it was issued through the media. Jeremy Wilson, a football writer on the Daily Telegraph whose reporting over recent seasons has proved he has better sources at the club than some people, had been sent out to St Louis, Missouri to see if he could get the man known as Silent Stan to talk. To Wilson's credit, Stan turned out to be anything but silent and, while watching his American football team, the Rams lose to the Baltimore Ravens, talked to Jeremy for an hour non-stop.

Most pertinently, Kroenke was effusive about Wenger. "I have tremendous confidence in Arsene," he told Wilson. "He is one of the great managers in the world. He is a great person and I love the way he handles himself."

Kroenke talked about Billy Beane, the famous San Francisco baseball manager who had just been portrayed by Brad Pitt in a fascinating film called "Moneyball". Kroenke revealed that Wenger was Beane's idol – not an obvious choice for an American wrapped up in the iconoclastic world of American sport. Kroenke said that Beane admired Wenger's "ability to spend money and extract value. That is what it is all about to be successful in pro sport."

Kroenke insisted to Wilson that he never interfered with a manager's decision over playing staff and said that the decisions over the departures of Fabregas and Nasri had been left to Wenger. "Arsene is big on the chemistry of the club and the best people I have met are big on that," he said. "It's not just about throwing money at it. You bring these guys in sometimes and the locker room gets weird."

Nasri and, before him Adebayor, were probably players who could have created a bit of weirdness in the Arsenal locker room which helped make their parting quite unsweet sorrow. Kroenke had, in any case, pin-pointed one of the basic ingredients of the Wenger Code – promote or buy players who can enhance the club's spirit and togetherness. It was an aspect of the Code that would become enormously important in the coming months.

So with blessings from afar, Wenger's October dawned with an immediate trip up the road to White Hart Lane on the 2nd. It was a daunting task. The team was getting its act together, no doubt about that, but Tottenham Hotspur, under Harry Redknapp's effective if quirky leadership, were starting to look like a serious outfit with an impressive line-up of top class talent. After losses to both Manchester clubs, Spurs had got their act together quicker than the Gunners and stood at 6th in the table with a game in hand over their neighbours who were still languishing too far down at 15th.

Wenger made six changes to the side that had beaten Olympiacos, the most interesting of which was the replacement of Frimpong as holding mid-fielder (Song was still needed as an emergency centre back) with Francis Coquelin, the young Frenchman who had looked like a very accomplished player on the rare occasions he had been called upon for first team duty. Loaned out to Lorient for much of the previous season, Coquelin now looked like a very useful addition to the squad, able to take up midfield duties or, later as injuries mounted, to fill in at right back.

The roar that greeted the Tottenham players as they emerged from the tunnel carried that extra pitch of fervor and excitement that comes with every encounter with the hated neighbours but especially so on this occasion. Redknapp's team had broken a long losing streak with that win at the Emirates the previous season and Spurs fans were now smelling blood – the blood left in the water from Arsenal's near calamitous start to the season.

No doubt there were some Spurs fanatics who were eyeing that 8-2 score-line at Old Trafford and thinking, "How many can we get?" But Arsenal quickly banished such thoughts by matching Tottenham toe-to-toe in a cracking, fast-paced duel that paid little heed to the warm weather. Sixteen goals had been scored in the previous three meetings between these two clubs and both sides had opportunities to add to that tally, not least when Van Persie laid on a great chance for Gervinho in the 28th minute. But the talented Ivorian who looks so comfortable on the ball poked it wide from ten yards out – a miss that left Wenger almost literally tearing his hair out. Unfortunately it would not be the last time Gervinho would freeze in front of goal as the season unfolded.

In the 40th minute Rafael van der Vaart was not so wasteful. Adebayor crossed from the right and the Dutchman chested down before lashing the ball past Szczesny. The Arsenal players appealed for hand ball but replays show that the ball connected with van der Vaart's shoulder more than his upper arm and the goal was a good one.

Arsenal did not buckle. Far from it. They came surging back to put heat on the Spurs defence and must have considered themselves a little unfortunate to be behind at half time. But Ramsey soon put that right in the 51st minute when Song's cross from the left found the Welshman a few yards from goal and Aaron rammed it into the top of the net. Not great defending but the goal was no more than Arsenal deserved.

Then fortune decreed that Arsenal would suffer again. Bacary Sagna flung himself into a tackle near the touch line and ended up hurtling into an advertising board. He was carried off with a broken leg. So Sagna was added to an injury list of defenders that already included Vermaelen, Djourou and Koscielny. And it would continue to grow in the coming weeks.

Carl Jenkinson came on and was soon put under pressure by the speedy Bale. In an effort to offer the youngster some protection, Wenger replaced Walcott, who had looked threatening on occasion, with Yossi Benayoun, blunting Arsenal's attacking options. Partially as a result of that, Tottenham started to seize control of the game but it needed another of 'those' goals to make the difference. Luka

Modric, who unlike Nasri, had agreed to stay on at White Hart Lane despite revealing a wish to go elsewhere, fired in a shot which was blocked by Song. The ball shot out to Kyle Walker, who had impressed England manager Fabio Capello while on loan to Aston Villa the previous season.

Now he was about to impress Harry Redknapp even more. Taking the ball in his stride, the right back looked up and let fly with a 25 yard howitzer that Szczesny was unable to handle. The ball swerved just as it reached the Arsenal keeper but Wojciech probably felt he should have done better. As for Walker he just admitted that it was a hit and hope move. "I just thought I might as well try it," he smiled. It is a thought that seems to enter the minds of Arsenal's opponents quite frequently. It was, of course, Walker's first goal for Spurs and he wasn't to score another for many months.

Szczesny did his brilliant best to make up for any share of the blame for the goal by coming up with a couple of great saves, one a flying leap to keep out Jermaine Defoe. But despite edging Spurs for possession 51% to 49%, Arsenal could do nothing to change the score-line. It had not been a bad performance by any means but that hardly made up for the fact that they left White Hart Lane with a defeat and another defender on crutches. Tough to take.

11

STAMPEDE AT STAMFORD BRIDGE

Once again, Arsenal had to return home and pick up the pieces. The loss to Tottenham was not nearly as demoralizing as that crusher at Blackburn but with lowly Sunderland the visitors a quick response was required.

Quick? How about thirty seconds? Gervinho, proving himself a better provider than scorer once again, emerged with the ball on the right hand side and passed to Van Persie. Right footed, RvP hit it straight into the net way out of the goalie's reach. Late arrivals had to ask what happened. Arsenal had gone 1-0 up, that's what happened.

Sunderland were all over the place and Van Persie, hitting the post and then putting a left footed shot just wide, could have had a hat-trick before half time. Instead they went in 1-1 thanks to a dead accurate free kick, taken from 25 yards out, by an Arsenal old boy, the Swede Seb Larsson after Mikel Arteta had handled. I can tell you that there is at least one ex-Arsenal player who was good pals with Larsson when they were together as Gunners who doesn't think much of him now. Doesn't think he knows how to treat his friends properly. But that is by the by. The mid-fielder is a fine player and a dead ball expert as Szczesny, beaten all ends up, will testify. (Word is Larsson learned his dead ball skills in the Arsenal reserves. Oh, well…)

Happily for Arsenal, Szczesny did much better from a point blank Cattermole header in the second half, pulling off a great save to keep his team level. They had been totally dominant but could have gone behind. A bit of artistry from Andrey Arshavin, on as a substitute, took him past John O'Shea and Lee Cattermole but his shot went wide. Another Arshavin shot was well saved by Simon Mignolet and noises of frustration started to be heard around the Emirates.

Then, in the 83rd minute, Wes Brown, who, like O'Shea a Steve Bruce recruit from the manager's old alma mater at Old Trafford, brought down Van Persie and the captain lined up to take the kick himself. There were too many occasions the previous season when Van Persie failed to do himself justice with his free kicks but not this time. Clearing the wall, he put the ball neatly into the near corner and Arsenal had a winning 2-1 lead. Despite all the chances the home side had created, Sunderland could have snatched a point as they launched fierce counter attacks in the dying minutes but Arsenal survived.

Not so Kieran Gibbs, who had gone off in the 53rd minute with a pulled stomach muscle. The fans would not be seeing him again for several weeks as the left back joined the ever lengthening list of defenders on the treatment table.

On October 19th, Arsenal flew down to Marseille for their next Champions League encounter at the vast Stade Velodrome which was looking a bit toothless as one stand was being re-constructed for Euro 2016 which will be held in France. But although slightly reduced in number, the Marseillaise were always going to create a passionate atmosphere. Arsenal's travelling band of just over a thousand supporters did their best to make themselves heard but neither set of fans could induce as much as a goal.

Marseille had beaten Borussia Dortmund in the previous round 3-0 with a fine display of counter attacking football but they were at home now and were expected to set the tempo. However, with Koscielny and Mertesacker playing their best game as a pair at centre back and Song working tirelessly in front of them, Marseille's speedy runners could never find a way through. Both teams had penalty shouts and when Jenkinson, in at right back for the injured Sagna, allowed the ball to hit his hand, he was lucky to get away with it. So lucky, in fact, that a furious Andre Ayew got himself booked for protesting.

As injury time got under way, both sides seemed resigned to the fact that they would share the spoils. Johan Djourou, who had replaced Jenkinson when the youngster became another defensive casualty in the 62nd minute, had other ideas. Spotting Gervinho in the penalty area, the Swiss swung over a huge cross and Gervinho instantly nudged the ball on to Ramsey. Making room with a couple of steps, Aaron let fly with what was virtually the last kick off the match and the ball was in the net. The stadium was stunned; Arsenal ecstatic and the points table re-jigged. The Gunners went top.

Neutrals might have felt sorry for the French team because there had been little to choose between the two sides but, back in North London, nobody cared about that. A season that had appeared to be on the verge of an early meltdown in the heat of summer was starting to look a lot better in its autumn colours and, for a change, it was defenders who found themselves picked out for praise as fans turned to Twitter to make their assessments of the match.

For @iammakki, Mertesacker and Koscielny were the heroes; @Ekogunner picked out Song and Koscielny for special praise while for @samfuller09 Koscielny was Man of the Match. In this cyber space age it is easy to discover what the fans think.

They were certainly becoming happier, especially after Stoke City were despatched 3-1 at the Emirates on

October 23rd – a day that provided a feast for the statistically minded. It was the 100th Premiership game to be played at the magnificent new stadium and the record before the Stoke match was strangely symmetrical: Won 66, Drawn 22, Lost 11. It was also the 150th match in all and when the second goal went in – scored appropriately enough by Van Persie – it was the 200th goal scored in the stadium's five year existence.

The victory, which lifted Arsenal to 7th in the premiership, a remarkably fast rise from 17th, was largely down to the introduction of Van Persie in the second half. Wenger had been joking in press conference that he was always telling himself he was going to rest his striker on Monday and then put him on the team sheet on Friday. But this time, he bit the bullet and started with Chamakh up front. Unhappily, the Moroccan, who had looked so promising on his arrival from Bordeaux at the start of the previous season, put a header wide early on and generally failed to impress.

As Peter Crouch had cancelled out Gervinho's well taken 27th minute goal by scoring from Jon Walter's downward header seven minutes later, changes were needed despite the fact that Arsenal were bossing the game. So on came the captain and a stabbed shot from Gervinho's cut back in the 73rd minute and a sweeping drive as the Ivorian crossed from the left in the 82nd, enabled Van Persie to say, in effect, "Look, this is how you do it."

That two goal whammy inevitably led to charges that Arsenal were a one man team. The first man to refute that would have been Van Persie himself because no one knew better where his goals were coming from. Without Walcott and Gervinho as providers his tally would have been nowhere near the 25 goals he had scored in the previous 26 league games.

Van Persie was certainly not needed for the Carling Cup match against Bolton Wanderers three days later. As ever, Wenger mixed youth with experience. Vermaelen made a welcome return from injury and found himself playing in a back line that included the talented young Spaniard Ignasi Miquel at left back and the 18-year-old from Leytonstone, Nico Yennaris, on the right flank. Both played well but Yennaris, in particular, caught the eye. Composed and efficient, Nico immediately looked the part.

However, Fabrice Muamba showed why some people felt he should never have left Arsenal by nicking the ball off Frimpong in the 47th minute, getting a return pass from Ivan Klasnic and rifling the ball into the roof of the net. Who could possibly have predicted that this strapping young athlete would collapse with a heart attack at Tottenham just a few weeks later and remain clinically dead for 72 minutes before his heart was pumped back into life? They say miracles do happen. If so, Muamba's recovery, which defied medical science, was one of them.

But we knew none of that on this particular evening at the Emirates, just the fact that Arsenal were 0-1 down and needed to do something about it. In a matter of minutes Andrey Arshavin had found the answers. A 53rd minute goal was followed with a pass that enabled Ju Young Park, the South Korean captain, to score with a lovely curling shot that gave Adam Bogdan no chance. Finally, the fans were offered some evidence of why Park was brought to the club. Unhappily, his goal scoring feats, so plentiful when playing for his country, were never to be repeated for Arsenal's first team.

So Arsenal were in the quarter finals of the League Cup for the ninth consecutive season, despite the fact that Wenger consistently fielded teams sprinkled with teenagers. In the beginning, critics accused him of belittling the competition. Obviously Arsenal supporters did not agree. A crowd of 56,628 turned up for this encounter and were well rewarded.

Not, however, as well rewarded as the much smaller but still sizeable number of fans who took the tube to West London, decanted at Fulham Broadway and streamed into the visitors end at Stamford Bridge. The mood was one of hope and cautious optimism. A run of seven wins in eight matches was definitely something to build on but Chelsea, under a succession of managers, had turned the Bridge into a fortress. Very few teams came away with a win.

Nevertheless Chelsea, with the young Portuguese Andre Villas-Boas in charge, had not looked infallible, losing 1-0 to QPR the previous week and Manchester United 3-1 at Old Trafford earlier on and many of the tightly packed red and white brigade, showing off their colours on a sunny afternoon, were thinking that at least a draw was on the cards.

Oh, did they get more than that! In a duel that defied logic, Arsenal could have gone 2-0 up after a few minutes; did turn a 1-2 deficit into a 3-2 lead; lost that and yet still ended up winning a completely crazy match 5-3. For a while both defences looked as if they had stopped at a pub on the Fulham Road and were still out to lunch.

Chelsea had already launched a series of attacks by the time Walcott hared down the right wing and laid on the most perfect pass for Gervinho who continued his worrying habit of missing sitters by stroking the ball outside the far post when scoring might have been easier. Within minutes, Theo's blistering pace tore through the Chelsea ranks once again but this time it was Van Persie who failed to make the most of his lofted pass across the face of goal and ballooned his shot over the bar.

It was astonishing stuff as the ball flew from one end of the field to another with both teams apparently happy to play kamikaze football. It paid off first for Chelsea in the 14th minute as Mertesacker's height still could not get him high enough to deal with a Mata cross from the right and, after grazing the German's copper coloured head, it fell onto

Lampard's thinning thatch and that prolific scorer guided it past Szczesny. 1-0

It could have been 2-0 as Sturridge burst through and found himself one on one with Szczesny. But he shot wide. Unphased, Arsenal kept going forward and, in the 36th minute Gervinho made amends for that earlier miss by dribbling through the middle of the one-paced Chelsea defence and, with Cech advancing, calmly side-footed the ball into Van Persie's path. Easy. 1-1.

Arsenal were looking forward to a breather and a job well done when, in the second minute of injury time, Terry got a foot to a Lampard corner right in front of Mertesacker and shoveled the ball over the line. 1-2.

If some people thought that might have knocked the stuffing out of the Gunners they were quickly disabused. With the Chelsea defence still looking like a bunch of Shire horses, Song had all the time in the world to send Santos racing away in acres of space on the left and, as Bosingwa, tucked inside, gave chase far too late, the Brazilian smacked a huge left foot shot through the legs of a startled Cech. Huge relief for Arsenal and particularly Santos who had been given a torrid time by Mata in the first half. 2-2.

Then, for me, came the turning point, the big moment of a match that had plenty of them. Walcott set off on another of his sprinter's runs but tripped and fell. Everything went into freeze frame for a tiny split second as defenders waited for a possible referee's whistle. But Walcott wasn't waiting. He was up on his feet in a flash and got lucky as a rebound off a white stocking fell back at his feet. A quick touch, another which took him past Terry and another and he was through. As he admitted afterwards he knew Van Persie was waiting in the middle but he just thought he had earned the right to take a shot himself. So he wacked it into the small space between Cech and his left hand post for a gloriously exceptional and stunning goal. 3-2.

Literally two seconds before Walcott had set off on that run, Stewart Robson, a frequent critic of Walcott's play who was commentating on the match for the Arsenal website, had said, "Now I wonder what Walcott can bring to the party." Silly hats and flying streamers and a great big goal was the ecstatic answer as the Arsenal corner erupted and grown men hugged each other in glee.

But it would have been stupid to think the match was won. Not this match. There was no script for this at all. In the 80th minute, the Chelsea substitute Romelu Lukaku pushed Santos off the ball, sending the Brazilian flying. But the referee ignored the incident and, seizing the ball, Mata sent a terrific shot flying into the top corner from 20 yards. 3-3.

Close up shop and be happy with a point? Joking, joking, joking. Arsenal don't play that way. Certainly not this Arsenal on this particular afternoon. They continued to attack and received the luck that the truly audacious deserve. Trying to take a pass from a colleague just inside his own half, Terry missed his footing and fell. "Couldn't have happened to a nicer bloke," was the sarcastic remark from the commentary box as Van Persie latched onto the ball and sped on, showed the ball to Cech and then, swerving away, neatly rounded him, to put it into an empty net. 4-3.

The jibe about Terry was referring to the fact that this controversial character had been accused of making a racist remark to Anton Ferdinand during Chelsea's match at Queen's Park Rangers the previous week. It had stirred a controversy which, months later, would see Terry acquitted of racial abuse in a court of law.

Judge and jury had not quite brought down the hammer on this argument but that problem was resolved in the 90th minute when Arteta released Van Persie who drove the ball straight at Cech and watched with glee as the ball bounced off the keeper's outstretched arm and into the net.

Van Persie's hat-trick and Wenger's 500th win as Arsenal manager. Could a day turn out more perfect?

The manager was obviously thrilled but he refused to get carried away in press conference. "We must remain humble and keep our focus," he said. "We still have some ground to make up."

But, he admitted that, psychologically, this was a huge step forward, not least because his team kept going forward and were justly rewarded. Wenger did admit, however, that breaking forward in numbers, as Arsenal had done to set up Van Persie's last goal, was the sort of thing that gave a manager pause. Smiling, he said, "At that stage you don't necessarily want to see your team go crazy."

But it had been a crazy match and while all the praise was understandably heaped on the captain, it should not have been forgotten that Walcott had laid on two perfect passes that should have put his team 2-0 up and then scored a very special goal to give them the lead. It was not a match that the defenders would want to pore over in detail. Better to wallow in the collective spirit that had brought about such a remarkable result.

12

PROGRESS THROUGH NOVEMBER

On November 1st it was Marseille's turn to visit the Emirates to see whether they could wrest the leadership of their Champions League group away from Arsenal. They couldn't. Critics kept talking about the frailty of Arsenal's defence but when the final whistle blew it had withstood 180 minutes of play against one of the best attacking teams in France without having let in a goal.

The only disappointment was that no one could conjure up the sort of strike that had earned the Gunners that last gasp victory at the Velodrome. Wenger had not made it easy for his team by resting Van Persie, replacing him with Park because Chamakh was injured. Once again the South Korean failed to score. So did Robin when he was introduced after 62 minutes and a good quality duel ended at 0-0 with Andre Ayew, who could have scored early in the match, heading wide late on.

So Mertesacker and the returning Vermaelen, partnered together for the first time in the centre of the defence, had held firm and Wenger could look at the group table with satisfaction. After four matches, Arsenal were still top with 8 points to Marseille's 7.

The following Saturday, West Bromwich Albion were the visitors at the Emirates and Arsenal found their scoring boots again. It was the Walcott/Van Persie tandem that opened the scoring – Theo forcing a half save from Ben Foster and Robin tidying up by putting the ball in the net. Vermaelen, making his first Premiership appearance since August 20th against Liverpool, celebrated by converting from a Van Persie cut back in the 39th minute and it was the captain who set up the third for Arteta to score his second goal for the club. More and more, the former Everton star was becoming an integral and skilful cog in Arsenal's midfield.

Norwich City had looked impressive on their return to the top flight but they were no match for Arsenal when the London side visited Carrow Road after another of those disruptive international breaks. With Koscielny filling in at right back as Jenkinson had been sidelined with a long term stress fracture in his back, Arsenal somehow allowed the dangerous Steve Morison to score after 16 minutes, totally against the run of play. But Van Persie ensured that the result bore some resemblance to the one-sided nature of the game by scoring from Walcott's cross in the 27th minute and again in the 59th when a lovely through ball from Song sent him clear. It should have been more but once again the skilful Gervinho failed to take a good opportunity to score.

The following Wednesday it was time for the return leg with Borussia Dortmund at home. The team knew that victory would ensure them of qualification for the knock out stages of the Champions League for the 15th straight year, not bad for the trophy-less side that so many people liked to write about.

There was still tension in the night air as half time arrived with the score at 0-0 but it took only four minutes to ease that situation thanks to Song's charging assault down the left that took him past two defenders before finding The Man and Van Persie at the far post did the honours as usual.

The Dutchman was in the right place again in the 86th minute when Vermaelen flicked on Arteta's corner and Robin finished the job.

It should have stayed that away as a pulsating encounter drew to a close but, much to Szczesny's fury, Djourou made a mistake to let in Shinji Kagawa who ruined the goalkeeper's record of not having conceded for five and a half hours of Champions League play. But it mattered not. Dortmund had been handicapped by losing their 19-year-old star Mario Gotze after half an hour and, for all their efforts, never looked like stopping this resurgent Arsenal side.

Van Persie's goals took his tally to 38 in his previous 41 matches in all competitions and afterwards Wenger offered that he had "never had a striker on this kind of run before." As this was the man who had managed Ian Wright and Thierry Henry that was some statement.

Writing in the Guardian, Kevin McCarra wondered how Manchester United and Manchester City, who had been having a very troubling time in Europe, were feeling as Arsenal became the first club in any group across the continent to qualify. Not too happy, one assumed but it was no time to be smug.

Within a matter of days Fulham were allowed to leave the Emirates with a precious Premiership point after drawing 1-1. It was a bitter sweet occasion for Vermaelen who scored an own goal when a hurried attempt at a clearance dribbled off his leg and into the far corner in the 65th minute and then redeemed himself by heading in Walcott's cross in the 82nd. The match was an exercise in frustration for Arsenal who found Martin Jol's team belying their lowly position of 18th in the table with the skill they displayed in being able to close Arsenal down in an over-populated midfield. Still, there were chances. Chris Baird kicked a ball off the line as Van Persie tried to maintain his scoring run and later Mark Schwarzer, the veteran Aussie who had so nearly become an Arsenal player the previous season, showed his reflexes were as good as ever by slapping away a close range header from Djourou. The draw ended a five match winning streak for Wenger's team.

The next set back was harder to take. A home tie against Manchester City in the Carling Cup quarter final was never going to be easy but Wenger refused to compromise too much on his long held belief that youth must be given its fling and included Miquel, Frimpong, Coquelin and Oxlade-Chamberlain, with Fabianski being given a run in goal. To temper that, the experienced Israeli captain Yossi Benayoun was handed the captaincy, Sebastien Squillaci played in defence and another international captain, Park of South Korea, up front.

The saddest aspect of the subsequent 1-0 defeat lay in the fact that the youngsters acquitted themselves very well. If anyone should have scored it was Park but, once again, he was too indecisive to prevent Costel Pantilimon making a fine reflex save. Chamberlain was right on target with a huge drive but Joe Hart's Romanian deputy palmed it away. For long stretches of play Arsenal were the dominant side and, on the night played the better football against a team that was captained by Kolo Toure and included the loudly booed Samir Nasri. But it counted for nought.

After several minutes camped around the City penalty area, Arsenal won a corner but a loose ball rolled out to the left hand corner of the penalty area. Koscielny, already in the box, was the first to sense the danger but his one legged lunge failed to stop Edin Dzeko latching on to it and speeding off down the touchline. Suddenly the break was on. Four blue shirts raced down field; Adam Johnson took the pass, swivelled expertly and passed inside to the deadly Sergio Aguero who had somewhat mysteriously replaced the defender Kolarov as early as the 32nd minute. With the smooth precision of a born goalscorer the Argentine swept the ball past Fabianski. It was the 82nd minute and although

Chamakh flung himself forward in a desperate attempt to reach a Gervinho cross soon afterwards, the game was up.

"I'm proud of them, especially the young players," said Wenger afterwards. "They played at a top level but it is a learning experience and it was naïve to give away a goal like that when you have a corner. It is very frustrating because we were the better team in the second half."

Frustrating and particularly annoying for the home crowd who had to suffer the sight of Nasri walking off with a grin on his face.

13

CHRISTMAS & 125 YEARS OLD

The team was now settled enough, despite a raft of injuries, to deal with a hiccup and get back to some smooth winning. Beating Wigan Athletic 4-0 at the Emirates on December 3rd got everyone into the Christmas spirit, especially as the name Van Persie did not appear on the board until the fourth goal arrived. Arteta from long distance; a Vermaelen header from a Van Persie corner and Gervinho, finally scoring when he placed a very deliberate looking shot into the net after Al-Habsi had partially saved from Van Persie, made it 3-0.

With Arsenal so dominant, it was inevitable that normal service would be resumed and so it was in the 80th minute. Walcott dashed down the wing and his captain was there to sweep the pass into the net. Goal celebrations were, of course, victory celebrations and Van Persie, knowing exactly where his goals kept coming from, hoisted Theo onto his shoulder like a sack of potatoes and pointed to the name on the back of his shirt. What a combo!

Inevitably, given that the top spot in their group was already assured, neither Van Persie nor Walcott travelled to Greece for the return match against Olympiacos and, with the Athenians still chasing a qualifying place, it was hardly surprising that they were more motivated. Goals from Djebbour, Fuster and Modesto with just Benayoun replying for the visitors, made it a 3-1 defeat for the Gunners who were not really firing at all.

All that was forgotten as the focus turned to a special moment in the club's history – its 125th anniversary. Suddenly people became aware that it has all started when a club called Dial Square was formed at Woolwich Arsenal in south London. A Scotsman from Kirkcaldy in Fife called David Danskin was obsessed with football despite growing up in a rugby playing area and he began talking to some of his mates at Dial Square where he worked in the Woolwich Arsenal munitions factory. The arrival of two players from Nottingham Forest called Fred Beardsley and Morris Bates inspired him to form a team. Membership cost sixpence.

As the official Arsenal history states, all this was very well but, at that moment in October 1886, the club had no name, no kit and nowhere to play. Adopting the name Dial Square for want of anything better, Danskin arranged a match against Eastern Wanderers across the Thames on the Isle of Dogs. We can get over Spurs fans' jibes about going to the dogs and record that the team which would go on to greater things won 6-0. It was Christmas Day and everyone repaired to the local pub, the Royal Oak, at Woolwich Arsenal station for an appropriately liquid celebration.

They had solved the shirt problem by asking Beardsley to see if his former team mates at Forest could help out, which they did, with a set of dark red shirts. Over the next few years things evolved. Wanting a more inspiring name, the club became Royal Arsenal and then, by the time it joined the Football League in 1893, Woolwich Arsenal.

After Danskin and before the arrival of Herbert Chapman as manager, no one had a greater influence on the fortunes of Arsenal Football Club than Sir Henry Norris, a

Kennington-born property developer who made his fortune in south London and, primarily, in Fulham. After helping to found the Cottagers and nearly amalgamating them with a new club that was about to be created at Stamford Bridge, Sir Henry noticed that Woolwich Arsenal, suffering from poor results and even worse attendances south of the river, had gone into voluntary liquidation. Taking over, Norris revived their fortunes to the extent that they finished 6th in the Second Division in 1914-15 – the last season in which football was played before the First World War.

A decision had been taken to increase the First Division to twenty two teams when football was re-started in 1919 so it was assumed that the two clubs which had finished last in the top flight would stay up and that the top two would be promoted from Division Two. It was then that Sir Henry went to work behind the scenes with a little skullduggery. He had invested £125,000 – a huge sum of money in those days – in the new Arsenal (the name Woolwich was dropped after the move to Highbury in 1913) and was determined to make the club one of the grandest in the land. Rapid promotion was required. So he persuaded the League chairman, John McKenna of Liverpool, to stand up at the Football League's AGM and make a speech that changed footballing history. With great force and eloquence McKenna argued that Arsenal, a team Sir Henry had settled at a new ground at Highbury in north London, should gain a place in Division One instead of teams who were, perhaps, somewhat more deserving. One of those teams was Tottenham Hotspur. No wonder they still hold a grudge. McKenna, apparently well briefed by Sir Henry, based his argument on the fact that Arsenal had been members of the Football League fifteen years longer than Tottenham. Some say his argument was delivered with so much conviction as a result of a little financial inducement from Sir Henry's well stocked coffers. No matter how it was achieved, McKenna's argument won the day by a margin of ten votes. Arsenal went up and, amazingly, have remained up ever since – the only club never to have been relegated out of the top flight since the First World War. And the only club to have been promoted without earning it on the field!

Those of an Arsenal persuasion might be inclined to call Sir Henry Norris a gentleman and a scholar. It is more likely he was a bit of a crook, but no matter. He got things done and didn't stop there – firing Leslie Knighton to install Herbert Chapman from Huddersfield into the manager's chair in 1925. Chapman turned out to be Arsenal's most successful and innovative manager until the arrival of Arsene Wenger. Maybe Norris was blessed. He had, after all, acquired the grounds on which Arsenal Stadium would be built from St John's College of Divinity. Oh, glory be.

I always find it interesting to look back on decisions that shape the future of great sporting institutions. …..Jones, the first secretary of the All England Croquet Club inspected some land on Addington Road, just off Kensington High Street when looking for a site on which to base a club that was planning to expand into lawn tennis. The suburb of Wimbledon turned out to be cheaper.

Similarly Sir Henry Norris inspected available ground in Battersea and Harringay before doing his deal with St John's College. He was concerned as to the proximity of Tottenham Hotspur, already established off the Seven Sisters Road at White Hart Lane and, unsurprisingly, so were Spurs. But the tube stop on the Piccadilly Line at Gillespie Road was considered a major plus because of the number of people it could decant right outside the proposed ground. How amazed he would be to know that the same tube stop provides the same facility for the 60,000 Emirates Stadium.

If David Dein showed commendable foresight in spotting Arsene Wenger as a future manager of Arsenal, then Sir Henry must claim similar kudos for persuading Herbert Chapman to move south and take over in 1925. Chapman was a true visionary and, before his sad death from pneumonia at the age of 55 in 1934, he had pioneered ideas such as electronic turnstiles, PA systems so that the crowd could be kept informed; boards with players numbers on them; the Highbury Clock and a change in the club's shirts.

The story goes that Chapman was playing golf one day with Tom Webster, a leading newspaper cartoonist of the time, and Webster was wearing a bright red sleeveless sweater over a white shirt. It was a look that caught Chapman's eye and, on reflection, he decided that the white sleeves would make it easier for his players to pick each other out in goal mouth scrambles. So the famous shirts were born.

But Chapman also had his eyes on Gillespie Road tube station. "Who's heard of Gillespie Road?" he asked. "It should be called Arsenal." And, so after considerable cost to London Underground, the stop after Holloway Road on the Piccadilly Line became officially called Arsenal. It remains the only tube stop named after a football club but many will have noticed that the name Gillespie Road is still there on the platform in old-style tiling.

Chapman led Arsenal to the League title in 1931 and 1933 but did not live long enough to see them triumph again in 1934 & 1935 to become only the second club up to that time to pull off a hat-trick of titles. So dominant did Arsenal become in the mid-thirties that no less than seven members of the England team that played Italy in a so-called 'friendly' at Highbury in 1934 were from Arsenal – goalkeeper Frank Moss, George Male, Eddie Hapgood, Wilf Copping, Ray Bowden, Cliff Bastin and Ted Drake. Far from friendly, the match was dubbed The Battle of Highbury as the Italians reacted angrily to the rough, shoulder-charging tactics of the England players with hard man Copping to the fore.

For today's younger Arsenal fans, history means Frank McLintock, David Rocastle or even Ian Wright. For me, it was the magnificent seven named above. I never saw any of them play although I met Drake, the great goal-scoring centre forward, when he was manager at Chelsea.

The heroes I watched were of the 1950's era - Doug Lishman, a sleek inside left who remains 7th on the list of all time goal scorers for Arsenal with 137 goals (five more than Van Persie) and his magical little midfield partner Jimmy Logie, a Scot with a twinkle in his feet as well as his eye. Welshman Walley Barnes at the back, George Swindin – a future manager – in goal; Les Compton at centre half and the incomparable left half and captain Joe Mercer were all larger than life characters to this schoolboy who had paid his one shilling and six pence to be able to stand near the tunnel as they ran out.

Many of these names re-appeared again in print or even film as the 125th anniversary was celebrated, offering reasons for the club's supporters, new and old, to look back on Arsenal's history with pride.

But, on December 10th, the Saturday afternoon that Arsenal hosted Everton, a club founded 132 years before, the name of everyone's lips was Robin van Persie. In fact, after scoring the only goal of the game, the lips of Wojciech Szczesny, a flamboyant character at the best of times, actually touched Van Persie's left boot as he bent down to kiss it at the end of the match. It was a funny but fitting gesture.

The victory had been hard earned, not least because the defence had been so hard hit with injuries that the club were clean out of full backs capable of being drafted into the first team. Sagna, Gibbs, Santos and Jenkinson were all out so the back four lined up with Djourou at right back, Mertesacker and Koscielny in the middle and Vermaelen on the left. Not ideal. And it got less so when Vermaelen was forced off with a new problem in the 83rd minute. Miquel, promising but barely ready for the Premiership, came on.

For a long while it seemed that fate might be trying to spoil Arsenal's party. They were running the game but couldn't score. Walcott, breaking clear with his pace time and again, unselfishly laid on a lovely pass as he saw both Ramsey and Gervinho running down the middle but they both managed to miss the opportunity. When Walcott had a go himself Howard brought off a great save. His knee had also blocked a Gervinho shot and so it went on.

Then in the 70th minute Song lofted a high ball from the right and Van Persie not only took it on his left foot but drove it on the volley into the goal off the far post. It was his 19th goal of the season and arguably his best. Perfect timing and technique. The boot, let alone its owner, deserved that kiss.

On the 18th, Arsenal travelled to Manchester for a pre-Christmas game against City at the Etihad Stadium. Vermaelen was fit to play but it still had to be at left back with Djourou on the right. But – for how long could this go on – another injury to a defender had a direct affect on the result. Obviously troubled by a groin strain as he walked off with the score 0-0 at half time, Djourou only lasted two minutes into the second half. His departure necessitated Koscielny moving into his place at right back, Vermaelen moving into the centre and Miquel appearing again on the left.

Every back line needs a minute or two to organize itself after a re-shuffle like that and Arsenal were given just five. With Koscielny nowhere in sight Balotelli found himself in acres of space as he charged down the left hand side, cut in and smashed a hard low shot at Szczesny which the goalie did well to parry. Vermaelen hooked the loose ball off Aguero but it fell invitingly for Silva who scored.

Djourou's injury had started Newcastle's famous come back from 0-4 down at St James' Park the previous season. Now his absence was to prove very costly again. No one is suggesting that Johan is the world's greatest right back but he had kept City's attackers quiet until his injury and would surely have been better placed to prevent the build-up to the goal.

But it was 1-0 to City who had, generally, looked the more dangerous team despite Joe Hart having to flick a stinging shot from Walcott over the bar. Hart was in action at the end as well as he dealt with similar speed and strength of wrist when Vermaelen lashed in a fierce shot from Arteta's well-placed free kick. Another Vermaelen shot curled just wide of the post as the Belgian tried to turn himself into a forward but it was to no avail. Arsenal should probably have been awarded a penalty when a ball hit Micah Richards' arm but City probably just about deserved a win which put them back on top of the Premiership, despite having lost at Chelsea the previous weekend.

Arsenal were away again three days later, this time at Villa Park where a Van Persie penalty in the 17th minute and a later winner from substitute Yossi Benayoun, heading in from Van Persie's corner earned a deserving victory after Marc Albrighton had scored for Villa after 54 minutes.

With Djourou out, Coquelin, the French midfielder, was brought in to deputise at right back and Frimpong took on midfield defensive duties as Song was suspended.

But the most significant happening, in some respects, was the introduction of Thomas Rosicky for Frimpong in the 66th minute – a typically attacking move by the manager. Like so many of his colleagues, the Czech captain had been out of the game for a very long time – eighteen months in his case – through injury but had been working his way back to full fitness but had found confidence elusive on his return to the squad. He had started only one Premiership game up to this point of the current season but, within a matter of weeks he would become an integral part of the side, eventually taking Ramsey's place on a permanent basis as the young Welshman started to fade in February.

But even a rejuvenated Rosicky could not force the breakthrough needed on the 27th when Arsenal were held to a frustrating 1-1 draw against Wolves at the Emirates. It was one of those games which had driven so many supporters demented the previous seasons when endless points were dropped with draws instead of victories that were there for the taking.

One of those supporters, was the Surrey cricketer Mark Ramprakash. "You tend to see the same mistakes again and again," Ramprakash told me. "At times we don't defend well enough as a team and then the opposition park the bus. I have a lot of sympathy for that because good defensive teams are very difficult to break down but it all becomes very frustrating."

As soon as Fletcher headed in as a shot deflected to him off Vermaelen in the 38th minute, Wolves parked a very big bus and Arsenal were continually denied as they tried to add to Gervinho's well taken 8th minute goal. It had all seemed so easy then but, as the match went on, it got harder and harder, not least because Wayne Hennessey joined the goalkeeping club who just love to show off their skills at the Emirates. The 6ft 6" Welsh international goalie brought off brilliant saves from Mertesacker, Vermaelen and, inevitably, two from Van Persie. But with Walcott missing this game through illness, there was no one to carve open the defence with sheer speed and even a red card for Nenad Milijas fifteen minutes from time could not help Arsenal find a way through.

For the second time in three matches the referee, Stuart Atwell in this case, turned down a good shout for hand ball after a cross had clearly hit Christophe Berra on the hand. But then this was the season when Arsenal would not be awarded a single penalty on their own ground.

On the final day of the year, Queen's Park Rangers did their best to ruin New Year's Eve by defending for their lives. With three former Arsenal players – Matthew Connolly, Jay Bothroyd and the recently arrived Armand

Traore – in their line-up, the Gunners style of play would have come as no surprise and QPR did their best to thwart it.

But before Arsenal could find a way through, the backline was disrupted yet again – Vermaelen going off and Coquelin, who had already filled in as an emergency right back, now being asked to do so on the left. It was becoming an unwanted ritual.

Happily so were Van Persie's goals. Latching on to a perfectly weighted pass from Arshavin, who had been preferred to Gervinho, Van Persie scored with the flourish that had become his trade mark.

That was it, 1-0, and a solid hold on fourth place to take into 2012. All the nay-sayers who had stated with such certainty that a fourth place finish would be beyond Arsenal in September had fallen silent, brushed away with the autumn leaves.

The statues being unveiled outside the Emirates complex were built to stand any kind of weather and Tony Adams, rapturously applauded by the fans at the start of the match, was on hand to see his image take its permanent place amongst the club's folklore.

14

INJURIES AT NEW YEAR

It was in the game against Everton on December 10th that Arsenal ran out of full backs. And it was not until they visited Bolton Wanderers on February 1st that they got one back. Sagna returned for that match but was out again for the visit of Blackburn Rovers to the Emirates three days later.

It is obvious that Arsenal suffered from having their wings clipped. Raiding full backs of the Sagna/Gibbs/Santos/Jenkinson type are crucial to their style of play and Vermaelen, often so effective as a goal scorer when he marauds forward from centre back, is not capable of playing the over-lapping role when he is at left back. And, in any case, he was frequently injured as well.

But, searching for logic is never easy with Wenger's teams and just to contradict everything I have just suggested, Sagna's return did not help Arsenal score at Bolton, the match ending 0-0, but when Coquelin stepped in for him for just one match, the Gunners humiliated Blackburn 7-1. Make of it what you will.

The facts, however cannot be denied. Arsenal's injuries are different from other clubs in numerous and alarming ways. There appear to be marginally more of them over all (although some clubs, like Manchester United hide injuries from the media); there are hugely more long term injuries than those suffered by other clubs (you can't hide a broken ankle) and, almost invariably, they seem to blight certain positions.

When Arsenal lost 6-1 at Old Trafford back in the days of Tony Adams, Martin Keown and Nigel Winterburn, none of whom were fit to play, the entire first choice backline was missing. Then there was the necessity to turn Mathieu Flamini into a left back during that season when Arsenal reached the final of the Champions League. For weeks, the club, having lost Gael Clichy to a long term injury, had no fit replacements.

But having to play with centre backs on the flanks for the better part of two months was exceptional, even by Arsenal's standards.

The irony of all this is that Wenger, ever since he introduced his new Code to British football in 1996, has been obsessed with fitness, preparation and the need for the best, state of the art, medical facilities. The Frenchman had been shocked at the training ground on which one of the country's premier clubs prepared for their matches when he arrived in London. A budget to build something befitting Arsenal and its reputation as a leader in the game was one of the first things he had asked of the Board.

And although Wenger is a man who likes to make his own decisions without too much interference, he was always ready to listen to the expert advice he had on hand in the person of Gary Lewin who left the club in 2007 to take up a similar physio's job with England. Everyone could see how closely the two communicated during matches and Lewin was never afraid to say, "Boss, I think so-and-so's dropped his tempo a bit. Could be the hamstring's bothering him." At the next opportunity, Wenger would have the troubled player off. In this respect not much has changed. Lewin's cousin, Colin Lewin, who replaced him, and the team doctor, Gary

O'Driscoll can get Arsene's ear any time they want to talk about a player's fitness.

Wenger, with his sharp brain and thirst for knowledge, knows plenty about the physical aspect of the game himself but he is always wanting to learn more. The Wenger Code had immediately demanded an end to the drinking culture and, if that only affected a few players, every member of the squad, all the way through to the juniors, found themselves on a very different, very continental diet. Fried food was frowned upon.

But no matter how much Wenger achieved in a short space of time when he arrived at the club, all the glory of the trophy-winning years up until 2005 did not encourage complacency. Wenger is a driven man, always looking forward, never satisfied with the status quo. The medical centre he built initially was terrific but medical science moves on apace and the Arsenal manager was determined to keep up.

So a new and vastly updated training facility was opened at Colney in 2011. About six years earlier I had been given a tour of the existing facilities but not before I had been asked to put a plastic covering over my shoes. It was that clean. I was introduced to Danny Karbassiyoon then a young hopeful whose career would be cut short by injury but who would take on a very important role for the club as chief scout for North America. Then I was shown the shallow recovery pool, occupied at that moment by a cheerful Freddie Ljungberg. It was all very impressive.

But in 2011, when the new facility opened, visitors invited by the club seemed to think there had been a major advance. Jules Wheeler of the Arsenal Insider website and Lois Lampton of AISA (Arsenal Independent Supporters Association) were given a detailed tour by Colin Lewin and Dr O'Driscoll and were obviously impressed. They talked of the new GPS system called Edge10 which was installed in 2009, allowing physios to monitor every player's condition through a medical data base that examined every muscle, ligament and tissue.

Wenger has a yoga teacher visiting every week as well as an osteopath for reflexology and a nutritionist, well versed in what is legal and what is illegal to imbibe. In these days of drug testing you can never be too careful. Acupuncture is also available to those who want it and throughout the building heat-sensitive windows open and close automatically to ensure that room temperature remains at an optimum level.

There are now three pools. A plunge pool with a temperature of 7 C to deal with bruises and swelling and in which players are advised not to linger more than five minutes. Another is set at 30 C to warm up muscles and a third pool with a floor that can be raised so that the water level rises or drops to whatever part of the body it needs to reach – ankles, knees or whatever. Add three full time masseurs and a fully equipped gym and the visitors were left thinking that Arsenal's precious talent was being pretty well looked after.

So why the injuries? Well, whatever some charts say about the number of injuries Arsenal have suffered compared to other big clubs, the fact is that on the soft tissue league they are about average. Where the graph gets ridiculous is when it singles out fractures. Then, unhappily, Arsenal top the league. Last season Arsenal suffered seven fractures when the norm lies between one and three.

None, thank goodness, were as bad as those suffered by Diaby, Eduardo and Ramsey in previous seasons (Gary Lewin says Eduardo's break at Birmingham was the worst he had ever dealt with) but they still sidelined players like Sagna and Jenkinson for months on end.

In an effort to discover why, Ix Techau, a dedicated Arsenal fan who runs the very-focused website Arsenal Report and tweets under the same name, went through a painstaking exercise, involving all manner of statistics, many of them provided by Opta and backed up by PhysioRoom.com.

Techau began by examining a theory put forward by Gilles Grimandi, one of Wenger's earlier signings from Monaco who now scouts for the club. Not unreasonably, Grimandi felt that, as Arsenal tended to keep possession more than most teams, they would receive more tackles and therefore more injuries. But the facts only supported the theory in one aspect. Arsenal were certainly tackled more than any other team in 2011-2012 which these figures show:

Arsenal   4,938 tackles received
Chelsea   4,423
Tottenham   4,355

However Manchester City were top of the possession chart but very near the bottom of the injury list. Swansea City, another team which kept the ball longer than most, also had very few injuries.

So Techau looked at something else – the number of congested fixtures Arsenal had to endure in their worst ever injury season of 2009-2010. There was a greater correlation between these sets of figures than anything else which means that recovery time was a big factor. If the team was consistently having to play matches just three days apart, bodies broke down more easily. Techau also felt that the fact that the previous season of 2008-2009 had also been very congested played a part because some players had suffered strain from excess play and carried those niggles into the next campaign.

But there was another graph which seems to throw some light onto the problem and it was rather embarrassing, maybe unfairly so, on the current staff. The last year that Gary Lewin was head physio at Arsenal the club suffered an average of 59.4 injuries August to August. The season after, 2008-2009, the figure was 76.3 – a rise of 28%.

It is impossible to know to what extent that is just a co-incidence but one thing is quite certain – Wenger would not have kept Colin Lewin, who is Gary's cousin, on the staff through sentiment or family connections. He is too hard-nosed for that. Obviously he has confidence in his physio department no matter how many knocks the players take. And if they have made any mistakes, he would not allow Lewin and his team to make them twice.

As somebody who has worked with him told me, "Arsene can make mistakes but he makes sure he never repeats them."

That trait was reflected last season when Alex Oxlade-Chamberlain, who made such an impression in the Carling Cup and Champions League, was given very few starts in the Premiership as the season unfolded. Spending most of the time as a frequently used sub, Chamberlain only made six Premiership starts. Why? Jack Wilshere.

Wenger felt guilty of over playing the 19-year-old the previous season and had been horrified to see what the consequences were. As a result, he was determined to hold back the Ox, no matter how strong he was. So Chamberlain hid his impatience, played as well as he could without ever getting into a rhythm but was still rewarded by the new England manager Roy Hodgson with a place at the Euros. If he goes on to have a generally injury free career he will have Wenger – and Wilshere – to thank.

Wilshere was, of course, just one of a whole stream of Arsenal players who had been put out of the game for months rather than weeks over the previous three or four years – Diaby, Eduardo, Ramsey, Van Persie, Walcott, Vermaelen, Gibbs, Rosicky, Frimpong and even the promising junior Conor Henderson who missed the first seven months of last season with torn knee ligaments.

Manchester United were also badly hit by injuries or illness last season, losing their influential captain Nemanja Vidic and Darren Fletcher for virtually the whole season as well as the dangerous Antonio Valencia for a long period in the latter half. Didier Drogba has been a frequent casualty at Chelsea, in fact he and Wayne Rooney have been amongst the most injured Premiership players along with Van Persie but neither of those clubs suffered so many long term absentees as Arsenal.

No matter how many pinches of salt are required while examining statistics, it is difficult to ignore some of the most official ones even though, as we have pointed out, some clubs are coy about reporting injuries. A UEFA study, published in 2011, came up with injury figures for the top 50 European teams. Each member of those clubs' first team squad were reckoned to suffer two injuries of varying kinds during a season. That meant a 25 man squad would expect to suffer an average of 50 injuries. Between 2002 and 2011, Arsenal averaged 66.2 per season.

Injuries to key players are incredibly frustrating just as keeping a vital player like Van Persie fit for an entire campaign – not least because Wenger rested him whenever he dared – is a huge boost to a club's fortunes. Is it greedy to wonder how many more goals Van Persie might have scored had he not only had Walcott feeding him from the wing but Wilshere spraying passes around for him from midfield? Futile now because our Red Robin has flown the coop and Jack was still trying to get fit as the new season opened.

But keeping more players out of the treatment room must remain a top priority for the coming campaign. Exactly how to do it remains an elusive science.

15

THIERRY HENRY RETURNS

The New Year sent Arsenal's fortunes hurtling into a mix of euphoria and despair as the team seemed to suffer from a weird dose of schizophrenia. Nine Premiership points dropped out of nine following defeats at Fulham and Swansea away and Man United at home would have plunged 2012 into a spiral of gloom had it not been for the seemingly magical return of Thierry Henry.

Of all the top players who had left the club during Wenger's reign, it had become obvious that the mercurial Frenchman had suffered from the greatest withdrawal symptoms. Even during his time at Barcelona he talked of dreading the chance of his new club being drawn against Arsenal – and, of course, they were.

But he had moved on to the New York Red Bulls since then and with the MLS in shut down during the winter months, the idea that Henry might be available to actually play for the club started to form in Wenger's mind after he had invited Henry to train with the squad while he was at his home in London. Wenger liked what he saw – a step slower perhaps but no less commitment, no reduction in skill.

"It wasn't planned," Henry insisted after the Bulls had signed off on a loan on the Friday before Arsenal were due to play a third round FA Cup tie at home to Leeds United on Monday 9th of January. "You can ask the boss. He said it himself. He was thinking about it but didn't talk to me and then it happened pretty fast."

Henry is an emotional person and it all bubbles to the surface whenever he starts talking about the club for whom he had scored 226 goals in 369 appearances. "Arsenal and me has always been a love story," said the man who was returning at the age of 34. "To wear the jersey again, I can only be honoured. People might think I am just saying that but when I left this club I cried. I haven't cried a lot in my career but whenever I do it seems that something is happening with Arsenal."

A few weeks earlier he had been present at the unveiling of his statue on the northern concourse and he cried then, too. And you can be sure there were more than a few misty eyes in the crowd on that cold January night when the great man stripped off and trotted onto the Emirates pitch, replacing Chamakh with the score against Leeds tied at 0-0.

It was the 68th minute of a typically rugged cup tie against one of Arsenal's oldest foes. Just ten minutes later, Song spotted the Frenchman lurking in a forward position on the left and, just as Pires might have done, he slotted the ball past the full back. Henry ran on to it and there was a collective intake of breath around the stadium. Surely not; surely the script could not have been written this perfectly. But it was. Throwing off the years, Henry took a touch, looked up and calmly as you please placed a curling shot around Andy Lonergan and into the far corner. 1-0 to Arsenal.

It was the only goal of the game and it will be enshrined in the club's folklore. It was like a re-run of what everyone had seen so often before but never expected to see again. Writing in the Guardian, Kevin McCarra said, "The movement and finish was so typical of the scorer that the episode would have been a cliché had it not felt so exhilarating."

It was certainly that. By the time everyone was breathing again, a crowd of 59,615 was chanting Thierry's name and the man himself was leaping around in wild delight before racing over to give Wenger a huge bear hug. It was an unforgettable moment.

With Van Persie sent off to Dubai for a brief family holiday to re-charge his batteries and Chamakh failing to grab yet more opportunities, Henry's return could not have been more timely. Oxlade-Chamberlain had fired in one of the 28 shots Arsenal had teed up but most of them had gone wide and when Coquelin, in at right back, pulled with up with a hamstring injury after 33 minutes, the worry was whether Arsenal's ever-changing backline could withstand the occasional Leeds breakaway. A youngster from Leytonstone, Nico Yennaris had replaced Coquelin to play alongside Squillaci, Koscielny and Miquel, hardly a familiar back four. But Yennaris' performance would have impressed someone else who began life in Leytonstone, a certain David Beckham, who was watching from the stands. Yennaris, who slotted in as if he had been playing full back all his life, when midfield was more familiar territory, was wearing number 56 on his back. In the Daily Telegraph, Henry Winter made the apt observation that fifty six could have reflected the number of full backs Wenger had been forced to use that season.

The victory over Leeds had been just the fillip required after an agonizing loss at Craven Cottage a few days before. After being held 1-1 when the sides met at the Emirates, it was important for Arsenal to get off to a good start and they did just that when Koscielny popped up to head in after 21 minutes. Gervinho could have scored in the second minute but fired over and then, later, hit a volley wide. Ramsey, who was commanding midfield, tested David Stockdale in the Fulham goal but the Gunners could not increase their lead and paid for it.

With the intensity level dropping, Arsenal found themselves being forced back in the second half and it eventually came as no surprise when Philippe Senderos headed down across goal for Steve Sidwell to score. Two ex-Arsenal men had just brought Fulham level. But worse was to follow. In the third minute of extra time, Bobby Zamora struck with a fine volley and Arsenal had greeted the New Year with a loss.

A visit to Wales was not going to be any easier. Since losing so narrowly at the Emirates in September Brendan Rodgers's side had surprised many critics by proving that they were able to withstand the rigours of the top flight with their quick passing style that was not too dissimilar from Arsenal's.

But they had built their success around a solid defence and had only conceded four goals at Liberty Stadium before Arsenal arrived. So Van Persie's fifth minute goal seemed to be a significant strike even though they were missing their usual batch of defenders as well as Arteta with a calf injury. But Ramsey caught Nathan Dyer's trailing leg in 16th minute and Scott Sinclair converted the penalty to make it 1-1.

Dyer finished off a good move to put the home side ahead in the 57th but soon after Djourou found Walcott with an excellent long ball and Theo chipped Michel Vorm, one of the goalkeeping finds of the season as far as the Premiership was concerned. It was not easy to get the ball over the giant Dutchman, but he managed it.

However, visions of a point to take home vanished within a minute as Arsenal were caught on the break and the prolific Danny Graham scored to secure a 3-2 win for Swansea – one that they deserved but which Arsenal should never have allowed.

It was a big reality check after the thrill of seeing Henry back in Arsenal colours against Leeds. The New York Bull, if one can describe him as such, had come on early in the second half but this time could not make his presence felt.

Worse, Henry had picked up a knock and was not available for the next match – the big one against Man United. A quick look at the bench for this vital encounter highlighted Arsenal's problems with injuries and personnel. Park and Squillaci? And the green, if talented Yennaris? In contrast, Ferguson had Scholes, Hernandez, Berbatov and a Park of a different stripe to call upon.

Even so, by the time the dust had settled and Ferguson's team had left for the North with a satisfying 2-1 win in their pockets, Arsenal could look back on a game well played, a game that showed no great gulf of talent between the teams, at least on the second half showing after United had dominated the first.

Ferguson had bravely opted for a 4-2-4 formation with only Carrick and Giggs in midfield and Rooney playing right behind the talented Welbeck up front. They had their own piece of injury misfortune as early as the 17th minute when Phil Jones had to go off but it mattered little as Arsenal were pushed back on the defensive and had to rely, time and again, on Mertesacker and Koscielny, playing their best match as a pair, repelling United's attacks. Some of the timing of Koscielny's tackles was brilliant and the German's long legs and quick reaction saved Arsenal when he hooked a ball away as it rolled towards the line after Szczesny had come out to dive at Welbeck's feet.

But the pressure told and when Vermaelen was a fraction late to sense the danger posed by Valencia in the 45th minute as a pin-point cross came in from Giggs on the left, the header went in and Arsenal disappeared down the tunnel 1-0 down.

The second half showed that there was spirit in this Arsenal team as a well as talent. Rosicky began marauding around midfield, offering glimpses of the form that would turn him into one of Arsenal's best performers as the season progressed and Koscielny built on his great defensive work to move forward and join in attacks.

It was another of the Frenchman's great tackles in his own box that started the move which led to Van Persie equalizing in the 70th minute. Koscielny found Oxlade-Chamberlain with a long pass and the youngster showed what a head he has on his shoulders by evading the obvious move and cutting inside his marker instead of going down the line. A host of United defenders were suddenly anything but united and Chamberlain was able to slip through the perfect pass on the angle to Van Persie who shot, first time, straight through a defender's legs to see the ball hit the inside of the far post and roll in.

It was a great goal and one of the reasons why Stewart Robson, in his post-match tactical analysis on the club website, heaped such extensive praise on the 18-year-old. "Oxlade-Chamberlain was outstanding," said Robson. "With his speed, his awareness, his tactical play, he just proved what a great prospect he is."

Rightly Robson, who can be a tough critic, insisted that Arsenal should hold on to the positives from this defeat, citing Rosicky, Oxlade-Chamberlain, the two centre backs and the teams' ability to make a real match of it in the second half as the prime factors.

But it was still a tactical mistake that allowed Man United to come up with the winner in the 81st minute. Valencia, playing at right back after the defensive re-shuffle but no less threatening for that, swept down the right, wrong-footed Arshavin who was trying, unsuccessfully to replicate his defensive heroics of this fixture the previous season, and grabbed the moment to find Welbeck in the area as Song made the wrong move and created an opening. The young forward rammed the ball home and that was that.

After winning 2-1 at Villa Park, a fourth round FA Cup tie at home against the claret and blues might have been regarded as a formality. But this was the Cup and, inevitably, strange things happened. Arsenal dominated the first half and went in 0-2 down. Richard Dunne climbed higher than any red shirt to head into the roof of the net in the 33rd minute and then, in the last minute of injury time, Fabianski's brilliant one handed stop from Darren Bent rolled straight back to the England striker who threaded the eye of the needle between the prone keeper and the inside of his post to stun the home crowd.

All season Wenger had been asked about how strong his team were mentally and if their spirit matched their ability. The answer came in a seven minute spell of the second half that turned the match inside out. Dunne lost his first half halo by bringing down Ramsey in the area and Van Persie converted the penalty. Then Walcott set off on one of his weaving, jet-fuelled runs down the right, fired point blank at Shay Given and before he could blink discovered that he had scored. Hutton had pounced on the ball as it rolled off his keeper and his lashed clearance hit the unaware Theo and bounced in.

So Arsenal, who been caught by a similar sort of re-bound when losing to Liverpool 0-2 in the first game of the season, got a belated pay back. It was lucky but the Emirates was prepared to accept anything on offer. It was no more than five minutes later when Koscielny, who was starting to enjoy his sudden surges up field, was clattered by Bent and Van Persie, going right instead of left this time, scored his 25th goal of the season by converting his third penalty against Villa in two matches.

Thierry Henry was on the touch line waiting to come on for another substitute appearance when Van Persie scored and suddenly found himself being engulfed by a celebratory hug from the captain. Arsenal were heading for a fifth round tie at Sunderland.

After three successive Premiership defeats it was essential that Arsenal got something at the Reebok on the first day of February and they did. But one point from the 0-0 draw should have been three. Van Persie hit the woodwork twice; had a shot headed off the line and Walcott, clean through – no surprise there – saw his side footed shot bounce off the underside of Adam Bogdan's boot as the goalie came out to challenge. In the end, Szczesny saved the day a couple of minutes from time by whisking the ball off the toe of Mark Davies as the midfielder burst through the defence.

It was good to see Sagna back for his first start since October 2nd at Tottenham but he needed time to pick up the pace again and could not be expected to be back at his best first time out. The team knew they'd blown chances and Arteta offered an astute assessment of the problems they were going through after the match.

"We have the talent and the quality in the side to do it but we have to show it day by day. I am confident because we train together every day and I know how good we are. But we have to show it every day and not every two or three weeks."

The Spaniard, whose displays for Everton and now his new club only emphasised just how good Spain's midfield must be to keep him out of the national side, went on to highlight the point I have been making earlier in this book. The margins are small - but they are vital.

"It's more about details to score," he said. "That would make the game much easier for us. We had chances to score and didn't. You are not going to get 15 chances to win a football match and, when you get it, especially away from home, you have to take it."

Boy, did his colleagues listen to him. Three days later, Saturday February 4th at the Emirates, the score was Arsenal 7 Blackburn Rovers 1.

No matter how bad Rovers might have been, Arsenal hit the net seven times, offering up a classic lesson in taking chances. Why one match and not the next? Football doesn't offer an easy answer to questions like that but the fact is that confidence has something to do with it and, with that part of the equation restored, Arsenal set off on another winning run that encompassed seven straight wins with 22 goals scored (including the Blackburn match) and six conceded. After a blip at Loftus Road, where they lost 1-2 to QPR, two more victories followed to bring the full record for this little segment of the season – February 4th to April 11th - to nine wins out of ten matches played in the Premiership, with a goal tally of 27 to 8. That's title winning form but there was a worrying horror story at the start of it – the 4-0 thumping in Milan followed by the Cup defeat at Sunderland – and then the sudden stagnation during the latter part of April and May.

During that run when Wenger's team were cementing their recovery from that desperate situation back in September, 18 points had been earned out of a possible 21. But the last five games brought 6 points out of a possible 15. Looking at the way they finished you could say Arsenal were fortunate to end up in 3rd place. But, surely, hadn't they earned it with that prior run of almost unbroken success?

It gets back to what Arteta was saying. You have to do it every day, or at least every match. And for a while they did. But not for long enough to push Manchester City, the winners by virtue of that extra time goal against QPR with almost the last kick of the season, or Manchester United. For much of the time, the ability and the spirit was there. But not all of the time. And that made the difference. The two Manchester clubs finished with 89 points each, with the title going to Roberto Mancini's team of expensive all-stars by a goal difference of +64 to United's +56.

That was way beyond Arsenal's capability. They earned third place with 70 points and a goal difference of

+25. But would they have taken that after crawling away from Ewood Park, numbed with frustration and defeat in September? Oh, you bet they would.

16

MILAN – A BRAVE RECOVERY

How does a team play as badly as Arsenal did against AC Milan in the first leg of the Champions League at the San Siro and as splendidly as they did in the return at the Emirates?

Home and away isn't a good enough explanation. The San Siro had seen Arsenal at their best in previous years. Inter had been taken apart 5-1 in front of the dumbstruck Milanese in 2003 and Milan themselves had lost 2-0 at home to the Gunners four years before.

Speaking some time after the 4-0 hammering suffered on this occasion, Laurent Koscielny admitted it was his biggest regret of the season. "The game just passed us by," said the Frenchman.

And after Arsenal had come desperately close to turning it around against all the odds at home, Thomas Vermaelen said, "We showed the real Arsenal tonight. It was not the real Arsenal in Milan. But it is very difficult to be consistent at the top level."

It was a mantra that Mikel Arteta would pick up on at another moment and Wenger, to be fair, had been banging on about all season.

In the end, Arsenal failed to progress and the fans were left to reflect on how one man, Christian Abbiati, the AC Milan captain and goalkeeper, had stood between their team and victory. Two great saves in Milan – one of them a candidate for save of the year – and two more at the Emirates made the score-line manageable for his team. But only just.

Everyone, from Wenger on down, knew that it would be vital to score an away goal at the San Siro and he sent his team out in front of a frenzied 68,257 crowd which included 5,000 travelling Arsenal supporters with this instruction ringing in their ears. "Be audacious!"

And they tried to be. Although a few early forays came to nothing Milan's cause did not seem to have been helped when Clarence Seedorf was forced off with an injury in the 12th minute. But that did Arsenal a fat lot of good. Three minutes later, Kevin-Prince Boateng found himself with space on the right and unleashed a great volley that beat Szczesny all ends up.

Milan continued to press and Arsenal, without the recently improved Mertesacker who had been injured during the Premiership win at Sunderland the previous weekend, were finding it hard to keep AC at bay. In the 38th minute, Zlatan Ibrahimovic, the unlikely sounding Swede who is never short on confidence, made sure they couldn't. Weaving his way down the left, leaving Sagna in his wake as the Arsenal right back appealed for off-side, the tall striker reached the by-line, and lifted the ball back with expert precision for Robinho to head in.

At half time, Wenger, presumably thinking that a bit of experience was required, replaced Walcott with Thierry Henry who had roamed Europe to such devastating effect in an Arsenal shirt during his halcyon years. But before he had time to find his bearings up front with Van Persie, Ibrahimovic went to work again and, aided by a Vermaelen slip, found Robinho in the centre. Measuring his shot, the

Brazilian who had never quite come to grips with the Premiership while in Manchester City colours, cracked the ball past a diving Szczesny.

A bad evening turned into a nightmare when Djourou, who had replaced the injured Koscielny who had hobbled off just before half time, got too close to Ibrahimovic and when his arm went up around the Swede's neck as both tumbled to the ground, a penalty was inevitable. Szczesny got the fingers of his right hand to the ball as Ibrahimovic did the honours himself but the Pole had little chance of keeping it out.

A score-line of 4-0 was looking like a catastrophe and Arsenal desperately needed a goal. To their credit, they went in search of it in some style and soon after Ramsey had headed over, the decisive moment of the entire tie arrived in the 65th minute.

Song broke down the right and crossed in the hope of finding Henry in the middle. The ball wasn't far enough in front of Thierry but, showing how his skills and imagination were still perfectly polished, the returning hero flicked the ball on to Van Persie with the back his heel. By chance or by genius, difficult to know which, the ball landed perfectly for the captain to pull back his left leg and unleash a high-velocity volley which arrowed away across the goal to the far left hand corner of the net.

The shot had goal written all over it but the problem was a giant eraser called Abbiati. Diving to his left, the goalie pushed the ball round the post and then immediately leapt to his feet, punching the air in glee as the San Siro roared in delight. Abbiati's reaction told the story. He knew just how great that save was and how important it was. Normally, at 4-0 up, it wouldn't have mattered but, in the Champions League where away goals count double, 4-1 is a very different score-line. With the score remaining as it was, Arsenal were going to have score four times and concede nothing just to stay in the tie at the Emirates. Had Van

Persie's shot gone in, the eventual 3-0 score at home would have taken them through.

Even then, there were more chances for Arsenal before the night was out. Wenger knowing full well what a goal would mean, sent on Oxlade-Chamberlain in place of Gibbs with Song moving back into the centre and Vermaelen switching to left back. The change galvanized Arsenal and as Van Persie burst into the Milan penalty area, Philippe Mexes had his arms all over the Dutchman as they collapsed to the ground. There were stark similarities to the way Djourou had felled Ibrahimovic but Mexes got away with it.

Still Arsenal attacked and it was Abbiati, once again, who thwarted the visitors when he brought off a smart save from Van Persie's downward header.

Roll on three weeks to March 6th and Arsenal, knowing full well what kind of a task they faced, took the field on a cold night suffering from the usual spate of absentees. Mertesacker had gone for the season and Diaby's return had proved to be very brief indeed. Now Arteta was injured and Benayoun was sick. A bench populated by the likes of Miquel, Jenkinson and Ozyakup looked a little green.

Obviously, with four goals needed before they reached parity, there was nothing for it but to go for the jugular which had proved a fruitless task in Milan against this very experienced defence. But, after all that sweat and toil at the San Siro, it took just six minutes to find a way through – and it seemed so simple. Oxlade-Chamberlain floated over the perfect corner from the left and Koscielny, unmarked, headed past Abbiati. Amazing.

Arsenal continued to pour forward with Rosicky, who only played after passing a fitness test that morning, gaining in influence alongside The Ox in midfield. And, of course, there was Walcott flying down the wing, crossing at one instance for Van Persie who thought he'd scored until Abbiati hurriedly kicked the ball away.

Next Abbiati made a flying save as Van Persie had another go and it would not take long for a team Milan could barely have recognized to force another breach. In the 26th minute, Walcott darted forward and Thiago Silva, trying to clear his cross, only pushed it straight to Rosicky who calmly threaded the eye of the needle, somehow finding space between Abbiati and his left-hand post.

Now the Emirates was alive and the noise must have been heard all the way up the Seven Sisters Road where some Spurs supporters probably had their hands over their ears. (Although, to be honest, some fans from both clubs are decent enough to support the other lot when it comes to Europe – at least grudgingly).

At 2-0, with the way Arsenal were playing, the impossible suddenly started to seem less so and The Ox made sure the thought didn't go away as his twenty yard run took him into the Milan penalty area where Djemel Mesbah took him down with Antonio Nocerino in close attendance. Penalty. And this time Abbiati couldn't keep Van Persie out. 3-0.

It had been a brilliant first half with Arsenal showing that they could not only match but totally outplay one of the best teams in Europe. But, as Vermaelen pointed out afterwards, playing at such a super-charged tempo takes its toll. Try as they might, Arsenal could not stay in the same gear after the interval and Milan, knowing they still had the advantage, concentrated on organizing themselves better at the back. Even so Abbiati was forced to kick the ball away again, this time from Gervinho and then, late on, came the final chance to take the tie into extra time.

Gervinho's skill got him into a scoring position and Abbiati, diving left, stuck out his right leg to cover that side, too, and the ball hit his boot off a deflected shot. The ball ran free and the tie's two prime adversaries, the Milan goalkeeper and the Arsenal captain, found themselves converging on it from about five yards distance. Van Persie got there first and was confronted by the huge Italian right in front of him. He tried a chip and as Abbiati dived one way, he stuck an arm above his head. The ball hit it.

Afterwards, the man who was obviously fated to thwart Arsenal's dreams, was decent enough to admit he was lucky. "I just threw up my arm instinctively," he said. "I had no idea what Van Persie was going to do."

Some people who weren't standing in Van Persie's boots suggested that he was just trying to be too clever with that chip. The captain rejected it. "I think the chip was my only option," he said. "The goalie blocked off left and right. But he made a great save."

The Milan players did not need to be told that they had been lucky to survive. Ibrahimovic said it for them. "No one of us expected the superb comeback by Arsenal," said the striker who had been almost invisible compared with his rampaging performance at the San Siro. "But Arsenal believed and they only needed one more goal. We were really lucky."

So, despite the disappointment, Arsenal's belief in themselves had been restored. Once again a big team – like Barcelona, Chelsea and Manchester United the season before – had come to the Emirates and found the Gunners firing on all barrels and far too hot to handle. By season's end we were wondering why the likes of Wigan and Norwich had not been similarly gunned down.

17

A RUN OF SUCCESS

After the shocker at the San Siro, there was really only one other major setback for Arsenal as they breezed through the cold days of February and March throwing equally cold water in the faces of their critics.

True, there was more frustration on the way because the team, come the blustery days of April, did not seem to be able to heed the words of Shakespeare's Cassius when he talked of a tide, when taken at the flood "leads on to fortune." A run of seven consecutive Premiership victories certainly created a tide that should have swept Arsenal towards a far better finish to the season than was actually achieved. Instead, it just helped to dampen the disappointment of losing in the FA Cup at the Stadium of Light precisely seven days after beating Sunderland on the same ground in the league.

The Premiership visit on February 11th had turned out all right in the end because the Henry factor was still at work. Arsenal had gone behind in the 70th minute in the most unfortunate manner – doubly so because it meant yet another long term injury to a first choice defender. Mertesacker, who had seemed to be improving with every match, went down like a felled totem pole as he tried to accept a pass from Sagna and that was the end of the German's season. There had been no contact. It was just that Per had twisted his ankle ligaments and would require surgery.

As Mertesacker lay sprawled on the turf, young James McLean picked up the loose ball, sped on free of interference, and scored with a great strike across Szczesny into the far corner. Lady Luck obviously took a bit of pity on the visitors five minutes later when Ramsey's effort struck the right hand post, dribbled along the line, hit the other one and went in. 1-1.

A draw appeared to be the most likely outcome until Arsenal's favourite new sub placed himself in exactly the right spot to head in Arshavin's pin-point corner in the 90th minute. It was Henry's 229th goal for the club.

Martin O'Neill had taken over from Steve Bruce in December and prior to this match, the team had earned 22 points out of 30 so this was obviously a setback for Sunderland but understandable in that they had played 120 minutes in a FA Cup replay against Middlesbrough three days before.

The shoe was very much on the other foot when Arsenal returned for the fifth round Cup tie the following week. The gloom of the 0-4 drubbing in Milan on the previous Tuesday still hung like a pall over the team and, no matter how hard Wenger tried to lift them and inject fresher players with five changes, Sunderland were too solid and rode a little luck with their two goals.

Kevin Richardson's angled shot in the 40th minute was probably going wide until it caught Vermaelen's arm and went in and then, in a strange variation of Ramsey's goal in the previous meeting, Seb Larsson fired in a shot which hit the inside of the post and ran across the goal line. Seeing the danger Oxlade-Chamberlain charged back but could do nothing more than help the ball into the net.

So, for the second straight year, Arsenal's FA Cup fortunes had foundered after tough travels abroad. Twelve months before they had found themselves trying to survive at Old Trafford after that agonizing defeat at Barcelona. This time a trip to Sunderland came right after Milan. Let's just say those two draws could have been kinder.

If you focus on the amazing events of Sunday 26th of February at the Emirates, nothing else really mattered. When Arsenal play Tottenham Hotspur, much of what has gone before becomes irrelevant. Of course the league table matters and the fact that Arsenal went into the match ten points behind Spurs who were in third place added some spice to the occasion. But as soon as the players run onto the pitch it becomes this great private battle between two neighbours whose fans spend enormous amounts of emotional energy through the season trying to do each other down. It is tribal, it is real and, for the people involved, there is nothing else like it.

What occurred on this particular occasion because it was so unlikely, so unbelievably dramatic and, ultimately, so euphoric for Arsenal fans across the world will remain in the memory longer than most. The score? Arsenal 5 Tottenham Hotspur 2. If anyone was mad enough to lay a bet on that score-line they have probably been asking David Dein which yacht they should buy.

That score-line becomes all the more unbelievable when one realises Arsenal went 2-0 down inside 35 minutes. The fact that both goals came against the run of play did nothing to assuage the fears of the faithful. Perhaps some clung to the painful memory of the previous season's meeting at the Emirates when Arsenal appeared to be in total control with a 2-0 half time score-line and proceeded to lose 2-3.

Incredibly, they need not have worried despite the fact that Lady Luck seemed to be riding a white horse in the 4th minute when Louis Saha's shot hit Vermaelen's leg and bounced straight over Szczesny's head and into the goal. 1-0 seemed a silly score-line because Arsenal, brighter, quicker and more inventive, had done most of the attacking. But 2-0 was absolutely ridiculous, not least because it probably wasn't a penalty. Replays show that Bale, who was not really in control of the ball, went down very easily as Szczesny came out to challenge him and, if there was contact, it was minimal. But it was given after consultation with the touch judge and despite the whistles and boos reigning down on the head of the player Arsenal fans hated most, Adebayor scored from the spot in the 34th minute.

Given what had happened to them in Milan ten days before, teams with less backbone might have folded at this stage but Van Persie's team knew they were playing well and that the score-line reflected little of what had been happening during the general run of play. So they set about doing something about it.

The response was simple and came from an unlikely source. Arteta swung over a cross and up popped Sagna to head in just before Bale, realizing the danger too late, tried to intervene. Perhaps it was an omen. The cheerful right-back with his ever changing hair styles had broken his leg crashing into the hoardings at White Hart Lane on October 2nd and now, in his third match back, he had thrown Arsenal a life line with his first goal for over a year.

With half time looming and Arsenal still pressing forward, Van Persie produced one of his best goals of his highly productive season when he collected the ball just outside the penalty area, pivoted away from the closest defenders and produced the most perfect strike off his left foot, curling it straight into Brad Friedel's top right hand corner. Suddenly Arsenal were level and the half time refreshments tasted a little better, especially as the football on view had been absolutely breath-taking. Pace, power, chances, half chances, great strikes, great saves – what an advertisement for the Premiership which, as ever, was being watched by countless millions in homes, bars and villages right across the globe. Even the neutrals must have been thrilled by this fare.

And, from an Arsenal point of view it did not take long for a pint of bitter to turn into a magnum of champagne as Rosicky, preferred to Ramsey for this match, burst down the middle, swung a pass out to the ever-available Sagna on the right and, as the return ball came in, nudged the ball into the net a split second before Friedel could grab it. The Czech's joy was unconfined as he spread his arms to let the roars of admiration flow down from the stands. What a turnaround but, incredibly, it only got better.

In the 65th minute Van Persie started probing down the inside left channel but he was well ahead of any support and the commentator cried out "Oh, he's going to have to do it all by himself."

Walcott had other ideas. Switching on the after burners as he rocketed up the pitch from a defensive position, one of the fastest men in football boots arrived just in time to meet his captain's pass and beat Friedel with a lovely chip. 4-2.

But neither Arsenal nor Walcott were satiated yet. Just three minutes later, Sagna, refusing to be left out of the action, lofted a lovely ball to Walcott who had timed his run perfectly to avoid the off-side trap and the England winger ran on before hitting a right footer straight across Friedel's goal and into the far corner. What a goal! What a come-back! What a triumph!

Neither the Spurs players nor their shell-shocked fans seemed able to understand what had just transpired. Harry Redknapp's side was brimming with talent and, until that point of the season, appeared good enough to give the two Manchester clubs a real run for their money. But suddenly the team seemed to slip down a gear and while their manager was being distracted with headlines that insisted he was favourite for the England job, the challenge petered out. Two weeks later, by the time Arsenal had beaten Newcastle, that ten point gap between the North London rivals had whittled down to one. It was a seismic switch in the fortunes of both clubs that would, in the final reckoning allow the Gunners to pip Spurs for that third place spot.

Arsenal had to travel to Goodison Park after the international break and it was never going to be as easy. But an 8th minute header by Vermaelen from Van Persie's corner was all that was needed. Everton were unlucky when Royston Drenthe's goal was wrongly adjudged to have been off-side but the win was gratefully received as it hoisted Arsenal into third place because Spurs were held to a draw at home by Stoke City.

Back at the Emirates on Saturday March 24th, the team moved into their home turf gear and took care of Aston Villa 3-0. Shrugging off the loss of Koscielny who hurt his knee in the warm up – Djourou stepped in – Arsenal were always in control. Kieran Gibbs opened the scoring in the 16th minute with only the second goal of his career and when Song produced one of his defence-splitting passes from deep to find Walcott, the Theo doubters were left with more to chew on as the winger controlled the ball with a magnificent first touch and slotted home.

The Villa substitute Andreas Weimann would have scored had not Djourou blocked his shot in the second half but if a little icing on the cake was needed the ever impressive Arteta provided it, lashing home a terrific 25 yard free kick in the 90th minute.

The victory took Arsenal three points clear of Tottenham who could only draw against Chelsea at Stamford Bridge – a perfect result for Wenger's team – and if a little extra morale boost was required, a seventh straight win proved to be the club's best run in the Premiership since 2007.

Unhappily, they couldn't quite see the month out. On 31st of March, the dreaded Ides hit and Arsenal lost 2-1 at

Loftus Road. Queen's Park Rangers scored two well taken goals from Taarabt and Diakite in the 22nd and 66th minutes while in between Walcott pulled one back by crashing in the re-bound off his own shot as it came back to him off the post. It was his 10th goal of the season.

Arsenal dominated the latter stages and threw everything at the QPR defence but they held firm in their packed and noisy little stadium down the road from Shepherds Bush and even the sight of Szczesny charging into their penalty area in the final seconds could not make them blink.

18

BEAT MAN CITY BUT JOB NOT DONE

Eleven months before, at the beginning of May, Manchester United came to the Emirates on their way to winning the title and lost 1-0. Now on April 8, Manchester City came looking for their Easter egg and never found it as Arsenal paraded their skills and won 1-0. But City still won the title.

So, in consecutive seasons, Arsenal were good enough to beat the eventual champions right at the end of the season. But never to be in contention themselves. Oh logic, where art thou?

On this occasion, Roberto Mancini was so depressed after his team had been outplayed for much of the match that he insisted City's title hopes had gone. "That's killed off our chances," said the Italian after doing his arithmetic. His team were eight points behind United.

In their two previous encounters, first at home in the Carling Cup and then in the Premiership up north, Arsenal had lost 1-0 and, with a bit more fortune, could have drawn both games. If you watched this third duel and checked with the video just to make sure you were not dreaming, there was no way City deserved anything. The score could easily have been 5-2.

But this wasn't Tottenham and City proved a little more resilient. They were unlucky when Yaya Toure went off injured in the first half but with a squad like his, Mancini should not have been too bothered. Toure was replaced by David Pizarro, the experienced Chilean international on loan from Roma.

The Sky Blues' chances came when Szczesny had to tip over from Aguero's header and Santos, on for Gibbs, kicked clear from the galloping Gareth Barry.

But with Rosicky and Arteta running midfield, Arsenal would have more than their fair share of opportunities. And the first big miss was comical in its absurdity. Van Persie smacked in a perfect header from a corner, except that it didn't quite go in because Vermaelen, desperately trying to get out of the way by thrusting himself into the goal, just failed the lunge forward fast enough. He was level with the posts when the ball hit him high on the back of his shoulder and bounced out. The Dutchman and the Belgian gave each other one of those "What the fuck?" looks.

Later Song produced one of his special through balls and Van Persie headed straight onto the base of Joe Hart's post. It was the seventh time that season RvP had hit the woodwork. Only Liverpool's Suarez had been denied more often. But does a shoulder count?

Man City tried to counter and had a period of dominance but the Arsenal defence held and their attack was soon causing problems again. Walcott hit the post and from the rebound Vermaelen mistimed his shot before the ball ran to Benayoun who missed yet another chance. Three in five seconds and still it was 0-0. Then Ramsey ran clear but miscued as he tried to curl one past Hart.

Something had to give and Arteta came up with the answer. Taking the ball off Pizarro, the Spaniard let fly with a screamer from 25 yards that Hart barely saw. It was a strike worthy of winning any match. To add to Mancini's misery, that time bomb called Balotelli flung himself all over Sagna in the dying moments and, as it was his second yellow, off he went.

I suppose Mario Balotelli is too good a story to resist but it was remarkable how even the serious papers spent most of the space allocated to the match talking about a player who, according to Daniel Taylor in the Guardian, put in a "chaotic, dangerous, bird-brained performance."

Taylor finally got around to admitting that "with better luck Arsenal could have won far more convincingly." In the Daily Telegraph Henry Winter was even more distracted by Balotelli's antics and he needed twelve long paragraphs before he was finally forced to focus on the team that had actually won the match. "Manchester City lost because Arsenal were hungrier, sharper, just better in design and deed." No argument there.

Both Taylor and Winter were joined by just about every other reporter at the match in stating that this was the end of City's challenge and that, barring miracles, the title belonged to United. They could not be blamed for thinking so. City – and, to the delight of the crowd, Samir Nasri – had been poor. Eight points in the second week of April is a big gap to close. They did it, of course, with the last kick of the season.

Boosted by this display of superiority over such a mega-rich outfit, Arsenal travelled up to the Midlands to play Wolverhampton Wanderers at their legendary Molineux ground where, as a kid, I remember them doing something very avant-garde – playing some of the first floodlit matches ever seen in Britain. It must have been the match against Honved and those Hungarian Magyars, Puskas and Kocsis who had humbled England at Wembley the year before that I recall because it was the first match ever televised live on the BBC. The date was 13th December 1954. That was the

Wolves of Billy Wright – later to become an Arsenal manager – at half back and Bert Williams in goal. Wolves went 0-2 down but came back to win a thriller 3-2 with two goals from Swinbourne and a penalty from Hancocks. Floodlight football. It was the start of something big.

The present team are not quite of the same ilk. Even John Lloyd, the former British Davis Cup captain who must rank as one of Wolves most fervent supporters, had been forced to admit that the departure of manager Mick McCarthy in February had probably sealed their fate. Arsenal certainly didn't help by strolling to a 3-0 win, courtesy of a Van Persie penalty after Walcott's speed had forced Bassong into error and another strike by Theo himself in the 11th minute.

Amazingly it was Van Persie's first Premiership goal since March 3rd – a long gap for a man who was to end up with 30 goals in the Premiership alone. Wolves at least offered Szczesny the chance to pull off one of his best saves of the season when he flung out a hand from a Kevin Doyle header but it never got the recognition it deserved because it didn't matter. Just to make sure the score reflected the context of the match, Song gave Benayoun a nice pass in the 69th minute and the Israeli scored. 3-0.

So Arsenal went four points clear of Tottenham in third place with this win which was their ninth victory in their last ten matches, including, of course a thrashing of Spurs and that impressive performance against Man City. So what did they do next? Lose at home to Wigan.

OK, so there has to be a reason, right? I mean we've established football as being an illogical game, riddled with daft results but aren't their limits? Well, let's try injecting some sense into the situation. For a start Roberto Martinez's team had slowly been turning themselves from heavy relegation candidates into a well organised, smooth passing outfit who had been unlucky to lose at Chelsea as they chased the game two weeks before and then went home and upset Man United 1-0. And I mean upset. Oh, was that a shocker for the Red Devil multitudes. So Wigan came to town on a wave of confidence and their chances of riding it all the way to another memorable victory were enhanced when Arsenal lost Arteta, their mid-field orchestrator, to injury in the 8th minute. Ramsey came on but the young Welsh captain was beginning to feel the ravages of a long season and could not pull the same strings.

A minute before Arteta limped off, Franco di Santo had scored for Wigan and before a dazed defence realized what was happening, Jordi Gomez was on hand to score as James McCarthy's shot re-bounded straight to him. Trying to atone from any guilt he might have felt over the goals, Vermaelen headed in from Rosicky's cross in the 21st minute but that was as much as Arsenal could muster. They battled and tackled and poured forward but this Wigan defence held firm and deserved their win.

It was a fine victory for Wigan but Wenger, sparse in his praise, focused more on his own team's failings. "It was frustrating," he said, with a face full of gloom. "In the second half I felt we lost condition and we didn't have enough productivity."

It was the team's third match in eight days but that should not have been an insurmountable problem. The fact was that, on this Monday night, Wigan looked a much better team than Manchester City had done eight days before.

By the time Arsenal had played their next three fixtures, Wenger was searching for a stronger word than frustration. "Diabolique" might have reflected his feelings a bit better. Chelsea 0-0 at home; Stoke City (never easy) 1-1 away and Norwich City 3-3 at home. The gap between his team and Tottenham was narrowing. It was sweaty palms time.

Draws and defeats at the end of the previous season; draws and the odd defeat at the end of this. The last ten matches of 2010-2011 had produced a paltry eleven points out of a possible thirty. This time it was better, 19 out of 30, but still the record of a team that was struggling to produce a Mo Farah like kick in the final stretch. So was the side losing focus; fading physically or getting nervous in the crunch? All those factors might have played a part but they do not explain how interspersed with all the dross, Arsenal won convincingly against Manchester United one season and Manchester City the next.

With Arteta side-lined for the rest of the season, Arsenal suddenly looked short of inspiration and generalship in midfield and as the match against Chelsea at the Emirates on April 21st petered out towards a 0-0 draw, the crowd yearned for another 25 yarder from Mikel to break the deadlock.

But the nearest Arsenal came to scoring was by hitting the woodwork, again and again. First it was Van Persie, moving his narrow miss tally up to eight, and then Koscielny, making one of his darting forays up field, who hit the post. In the dying moments, Cahill brought down Van Persie in the box but referee Mike Dean said no penalty. No surprise there. Referees had been saying no to Arsenal penalty appeals at home all season but if there was one ref who might have been expected to go with a penalty appeal it was Dean who, come seasons end, had awarded more penalties, twelve, than anyone else. Incredibly the Gunners went through the entire Premiership season at home without being awarded a single penalty. In fact, they ended up very near the bottom of the overall penalties league, having received just three. Only Sunderland, Norwich City and QPR with two each were below them.

No prizes for guessing the team who got the referees to point to the spot most frequently. Manchester United! They got eleven, three more than Manchester City and, surprisingly, Blackburn Rovers who both received eight.

Logically – sorry to have to use that word again – it is teams with attackers who combine lightning speed with tricky ball skills who earn the penalties because bamboozled defenders are simply late with the tackle. With Van Persie, Walcott, Gervinho and Arshavin, Arsenal are not exactly short of those but it made no difference. If referees are ever swayed by the baying of the crowd at other grounds, they are stone deaf at the Emirates.

Anyway, let's be charitable. Chelsea had fought hard for their point under difficult circumstances. They were in the middle of a run that required them to play four matches in nine days across three competitions and, given a new spirit by the promoted deputy manager Roberto di Matteo, they soldiered on to that unforeseen triumph in the Champions League.

Arsenal went up to Stoke on the 28th and might have won that match, too, if the referee had decided that Benayoun had been brought down illegally late in the game. But he didn't and Arsenal had to content themselves with a 1-1 result which, at the Britannia Stadium, is never easily earned. Peter Crouch's ninth minute goal did nothing to persuade the new England manager Roy Hodgson that the bean-pole striker might be useful at the Euros – after all, he only scores goals – but it was not long before an accurate Rosicky cross enabled Van Persie to level.

When Benayoun found himself free on the left in the second minute of the home match with Norwich City on May 5th and sent a lovely shot across Ruddy and into the far corner, Arsenal seemed set for some fun in the spring sunshine. Unhappily, Szczesny came up with one of his worst mistakes of the season in allowing an innocuous looking shot from Wesley Hoolahan to slip through his hands just ten minutes later and when the prolific Grant Holt needed a deflection off Gibbs to add another, the Canaries were chirping.

It needed Van Persie, who else, to silence them momentarily in the second half when Song, in the 72nd minute, offered another of those passes that makes Robin sing and then the Dutchman scored again off a rebound in the 80th to put Arsenal 3-2 up. However, Norwich were intent on proving they were worthy of their place in the Premiership and when Steve Morison broke down the right five minutes later, he was too quick for everyone and slammed a great shot into the far corner.

The ending virtually wrote itself. With just a couple of minutes left, Kyle Naughton brought down Van Persie but, of course, referee Anthony Taylor didn't want to know. So for the third consecutive game, Arsenal had been denied a penalty in the last minutes, any one of which, if converted, would probably have won them the match.

There was no time to worry about that as Wenger took his team to the Hawthorns where West Bromwich Albion were preparing to say goodbye to Roy Hodgson who had enjoyed a brief but popular stay at the club. For Hodgson's team the main incentive was to give their manager a good send off to the England job. Arsenal's was rather more nerve racking. To ensure direct entry into the Champions League the following season, they had to win, unless, of course, Tottenham lost.

To say they needed a little luck to achieve their aim would be an understatement but then you could say they were owed a little. For once, just for once, Arsenal found themselves confronted by a goalkeeper who, instead of playing a blinder, actually did his best to score goals for them.

Poor Marton Fulop. The Hungarian had not started a Premiership match since the beginning of the season and would not have started this one had Ben Foster not hurt his groin in training the previous day. So Fulop played and flopped spectacularly. The match was barely four minutes old when Fulop made a total mess of receiving a back pass from Olsson, allowing the ball to bobble around his feet which is never a good thing to do when a predator like Yossi

Benayoun is lurking. In a flash Benayoun whipped the ball off the dithering keeper and put it in West Brom's net.

The Arsenal defence, so water tight against Man City, Wolves and Chelsea, then went into its end of season "oh, dear me, who was supposed to be marking him?" routine as first Shane Long and then Graham Dorrans was allowed to burst through and score. Arsenal 1-2 down; Spurs winning; not good.

But if Santos had not been paying attention to his defensive duties – difficult when you are playing mostly in the opposition's half – the Brazilian made amends after 28 minutes when he smashed a great shot just inside Fulop's left post. Some people thought the Hungarian should have done better but let's give the guy a break. It was nothing to what was to come next. Going up for a routine cross that he might have caught, Fulop went for the punch which was a reasonable choice except for one embarrassing fact – instead of punching out, he punched it straight towards his own goal where Koscielny, whose natural expression tends to be one of mild surprise, looked quite amazed at being given the opportunity to prod the ball into the net.

At 3-2 up Arsenal were Europe bound but it was not over yet. Deciding that he really did need a left back out there, Wenger sent on Kieran Gibbs which allowed Santos to play where he had been playing anyway, somewhere in the left of midfield, and it was the manager's final master stroke of the season. In the dying seconds, Billy Jones broke clear and Gibbs came up with a quite brilliant sliding tackle to prevent a certain goal. Is one tackle worth twenty five million pounds? You could say that one was.

So Arsenal had won their "trophy-by-proxy" as Barney Ronay described it in the Guardian. He was referring to the club's achievement of getting into the Champions League for the 15th straight season which was worth some sort of trophy, especially after a campaign that had seen them written off for a top four finish in the autumn. To finish third was quite remarkable and, of course, it was made all the sweeter by the fact that it was Spurs, once again, who had been pipped at the post. It had happened in 2006 when some dodgy lasagne laid half the Tottenham team low before a match they needed to win and couldn't. Arsenal were the beneficiaries then, too.

Tottenham fans had every reason to feel aggrieved and even some of the Arsenal fraternity could understand why. Finishing fourth is normally good enough to put a team into the qualifying rounds for the Champions League, providing another club from that country does not win the whole thing. And, of course, against all the odds, Chelsea did just that with astonishing victories over Barcelona in the semi-final and Bayern Munich in the final. So it was the Europa League for Tottenham but not for Harry Redknapp. He was fired.

The celebrations at the Hawthorns continued awhile. Not only were the home fans intent on giving Roy Hodgson a good send off but Arsenal were also saying goodbye to one of their most popular and longest-serving stalwarts in Wenger's assistant manager Pat Rice. The former Northern Ireland international who had appeared at right-back for the club on 528 occasions was finally retiring, having stayed on for another season at Wenger's request.

Always in Arsene's shadow but the loudest voice in the dressing room before matches according to Johan Djourou, Rice was chaired around the ground to the visitors' corner where he received a deserving accolade from the crowd in red and white. Starting work at a greengrocers shop on Gillespie Road as a teenager in the 1960's, Rice started in Arsenal's Youth team and, along with the former secretary Ken Friar, whose name now adorns the North Bridge at Ashburton Grove, went on to give Arsenal as long a period of dedicated service as anyone in the club's history. Before leaving for a spell at Watford, Rice had appeared in five FA Cup Finals, including captaining the team when they defeated Manchester United in 1979. Pat returned to Arsenal in 1984 as Youth team coach and was briefly Arsenal's caretaker manager as they waited for Wenger to arrive from Japan in 1996. Immediately he slotted in at Arsene's side and received, when his retirement was announced, a heartfelt tribute from his boss.

"Pat is a true Arsenal legend," said Wenger who gave his deputy a big hug at the end of the match. "He has committed almost his whole life to Arsenal Football Club which shows huge loyalty and devotion. I will always be indebted to him for his expert insight into Arsenal and football as a whole."

But the final acts of this incredible season were not just about Rice. As the players departed Robin van Persie turned and came back for a final wave. How final? Most observers in the press box felt it was very final and, a few weeks later, they were proved right.

19

AND SO TO THE FUTURE

As I write Arsenal fans are holding their breath. By the time you read this, they will have released it either with a gust of despair or a cry of joy.

Amusement at Robin van Persie's lack of impact when he came on as a substitute in those Manchester United colours at Goodison Park and could do nothing to prevent Everton claiming a well-deserved 1-0 victory may have turned to disgust in the intervening weeks because it is hard to see RvP not linking with Wayne Rooney to score quite a few goals for Ferguson's team. Unless he gets injured.

But even though most Arsenal fans seemed to be resigning themselves that an intake of around £24 million for a 29-year-old with a year on his contract was a good deal, there was still a lot of indignation, to use a polite word, over the fact that the club's captain has chosen, specifically, to go to Arsenal's most dangerous rivals.

"I always listen to the child inside me and it screamed 'Manchester United'" Van Persie said by way of explanation.

That stuck in the throat. Leaving for Juventus or another top team in Europe would have been acceptable to

165

the majority but United? It drove a lot of people crazy, not least Piers Morgan, the ex-Daily Mirror editor and CNN talk show host who is a fanatical Gooner and has actually made Arsenal quite well known in America by talking up the club whenever he gets the opportunity. Morgan, who has over a million followers on Twitter, was soon tweeting away, vitriol dripping from every word. "A Sickening Betrayal", he called it to begin with and other tweets soon followed.

"Funny, I really thought Van Persie was different. But he turned out to be just another mercenary, heartless, selfish little shit."

And this: "Well done, Ivan Gazidis, a great bit of business – selling Arsenal's top player to our bitterest rivals. Shame on you and the whole Board."

Morgan has a bigger audience than most but he was not alone in voicing those kinds of sentiments. A gentleman called Giles from Bath phoned into Tom Watt's Fans' Forum a few days after the Sunderland game and seemed to be speaking for many when he said, "It would have been fine for Van Persie to go abroad. But for him to go to our biggest rivals – I really think someone crossed the line with that. It's unacceptable. Someone, Arsene, Ivan (Gazidis), Robin really crossed the line."

Giles went on to say, "I don't know of any business model that says you should sell your best and most productive asset to a competitor. Fans always have to suck it up, year after year. Selling to Manchester United for whatever price isn't good enough. When I first heard about it, you had to talk me off the ledge."

I can't argue with any of that but sources from inside the club insist they had no option. Van Persie was listening to that inner child and had his heart set on Old Trafford.

"You could say that selling to United is never good business," said Tom Watt. "But once a player gets it into his head he wants to leave, it's better to get him off the premises."

There were similarities with the decision to sell Alex Song to Barcelona for three instalments of £5 million each. Song, through his agent Darren Dein, had started agitating to have his contract renewed, and presumably, improved, towards the end of last season even though there were over two years to go on the one he had. Surprisingly, for someone who seemed such a popular and integral part of the team, Song started to sulk. His defensive work slipped in the last few games and, from all accounts, he drove Wenger's new assistant coach, Steve Bould, nuts at the pre-season training camp in Germany by turning up late and not trying. It was very unprofessional and that sort of behaviour certainly won't be tolerated at the Nou Camp.

I can imagine Bould delivered a similar sort of speech to the one I witnessed when I took my son Ashley for a couple of days training at Arsenal's Youth Academy at Hale End a few years back. Ashley, who was thrown in with the Under Elevens, was having his sandwich in the canteen at lunchtime when a few of the boys started throwing their food at each other. It was harmless stuff but, unfortunately for them, Roy Massey, the Academy Manager and assistant coach to Liam Brady and David Court, walked in and caught them at it.

Everyone was marched outside and told to sit down in a circle on one of three pitches that surround the full-size indoor pitch which makes this training ground so special for youngsters. A few of us parents trudged out to listen.

Perhaps Roy will forgive me if I paraphrase him here because I did not take notes but the gist of his little speech was this: "Now you lot, listen to me. We have standards at Arsenal Football Club and throwing your food around doesn't meet them. It is a PRIVILEGE for you to be here and it is a privilege that can easily be taken away. It is a PRIVILEGE for me to be here working for Arsenal and it is not one I take lightly. You see those boys training over there? They are the 13 and 14 year olds who are already professional enough to be getting ready for Arsenal's reserve teams. They don't want to be around silly kids who don't know how to behave. So shape up or you'll be out of here."

Massey had laid it on thick with a purpose. He wanted to make a point and wasn't as angry as he sounded. As he walked past us, he winked. "Hope they got the message," he muttered.

The memory dovetailed into a comment made by another caller to the Fans Forum, a Jonathan from Ilford. He pointed out that it was disappointing to go on losing players after they had been improved by Wenger and his teachings. "Wenger is better than anyone in the world at improving players because he coaches them properly and he needs to get more credit for the work he does with the players," said Jonathan. "Every player who comes here leaves a better player. That's not true with Ferguson. Look at Carrick and Anderson and Nani. And why doesn't Mancini coach Johnson and Savic into better players instead of trying to find ready-made replacements in the transfer market?"

John Cross of the Daily Mirror, sitting in with Watt, quickly picked up on that. "Song is a great example of that. When I first saw him at Fulham he had to be substituted at half time because he was so bad the Arsenal fans were giving him a tough time. But then Arsene sent him to Charlton, brought him back, and turned him into this player who gave eleven assists last season. It was amazing what he did with Song."

That set me thinking about the players who had come and gone during Wenger's reign. Had the Wenger Code done them anything but good? Run down the list: Patrick Vieira, Freddie Ljungberg, Robert Pires, Thierry Henry, Emmanuel Petit, Kolo Toure, Gilberto, Mathieu Flamini and Alexander Hleb were all gratefully received by other clubs because they had the Wenger stamp of excellence. Some might have been well established on arrival but they all became better footballers under Wenger. And it is the same for those still at the club – Bacary Sagna, Wojciech Szczesny, Theo Walcott, Kieran Gibbs, Francis Coquelin and Alex Oxlade-Chamberlain are all improving because they have been forced to adhere to the all-embracing Code that encompasses so much more than just kicking a football.

Of course there are those who pass through the Academy, listen to Massey's exhortations; try their butts off and just aren't quite good enough. But they all go off to other clubs with the solid foundation that enables them to improve as they gain experience in the Premier League or Championship.

Has Wenger had some failures? Inevitably, but I can only think of a couple who showed no marked improvement before they left. Both were English – Francis Jeffers, who proved to be more of a rabbit than a fox in the box at Highbury and Richard Wright, who was already an England international goalkeeper when he arrived from Ipswich Town but found the Arsenal stage too big for him.

Interestingly, Eduardo, the little Brazilian-born Croatian striker who had suffered that ghastly broken leg at Birmingham, was harping on the same subject when he was interviewed after the news about Van Persie and Song had come through. Obviously still caring for the club for whom he had scored 22 goals, Eduardo expressed his disappointment that Arsenal were finding it impossible to hold on to their stars.

"Every player comes to Arsenal as a simple player and Arsenal make them into a big player," he said. "Buy player, make them into class player; sell them next year. It is not good. They are always in the same place."

Now, isn't that the truth.

If it is mind-bendingly frustrating for the fans and all who love Arsenal, what must it be like for the maestro himself? If ever someone lived, breathed and probably dreamt the sport, it is Arsene Wenger. I always think it must be emotionally difficult for great artists to create a masterpiece and then have to sell it. But at least The Scream never came back and scored two goals against its creator, Edvard Munch. Not that the Norwegian, a bar brawler in his drinking days, would have taken it lying down. Eduardo, who didn't really want to leave Arsenal, scoring a winner for his new club Shakhtar Donetsk, in the Champions League was bad enough but what if Van Persie sticks one in for Man U at the Emirates. How will Wenger feel then?

He is, of course, an emotional man but a tough one, too and would no doubt find some ironic comment, accompanied by that small, mischievous smile which crosses his face whenever he talks to the media. It is one of the skills he has learned since setting off on his long and hugely successful path that began in his home town of Duttlenheim in Alsace. When he started playing for FC Duttlenheim it was obvious he was never going to be a world class player but then Alex Ferguson, although probably a whole level up from Wenger, was never a Michael Laudrup, either.

But, as he began his playing career, Wenger was already well equipped with knowledge of the game. He had spent hours listening to the local players talk tactics while growing up at his parents bistro, Le Croix d'Or, and insisted that the rough and tumble ambiance offered a free and early education into the way adults behaved. As a course in man management, it was probably priceless.

Our intrepid publisher, Greg Adams, turned himself into a bit of a reporter in August when he stopped off at Duttlenheim on his way to London from his home in Germany. After finding Le Croix d'Or (no longer in the family and now renamed La Baite) he went in search of the local football ground and found a local man, Claude Kocher, marking out the pitch.

Striking up a conversation in French, Greg mentioned Arsene Wenger and Monsieur Kocher replied that he'd been the goalkeeper alongside Wenger in 1968. Turning around he pointed to a man in the distance and said, "And he played on the wing."

The man in the distance was club President, Joel Muller who arrived a few minutes later and introduced himself. Greg mentioned that he was a big Arsenal fan and received a quizzical look from Joel. "Who?", he said. "Arsenal, the English football team," Greg repeated, wondering if his accent was causing the confusion. "Sorry, I don't know them," said Joel feigning ignorance before Greg realised he was being teased and gave the club President a friendly punch on the arm.

Following Joel Muller into the clubhouse Greg came face to face with montage of photographs celebrating a trip by FC Duttlenheim to Highbury in 2004. Arsene Wenger's picture was the centrepiece.

Muller declared, "Arsene was a good player when he was playing for FC Duttlenheim because he had me playing outside him on the left wing!" It was all very jolly and Greg came away feeling that the Wenger legacy, with all the old team photos on the walls, was alive and well in his little home town.

His legacy at Arsenal is safe, too. The statue is already there and there should be many more episodes in a life's work to add to the tale. After such a long barren spell, with all his studious work getting him "so close, so close" it is time for the Wenger Code to work its magic again and burnish the legend of the unique and remarkable institution that is Arsenal Football Club.

EPILOGUE

The irrational passion that has fired the motivation to write this book was born over sixty years ago. I grew up on the exploits of Pete Goring, Reg Lewis, Doug Lishman and wee Jimmy Logie with big Les Compton at centre half. Joe Mercer was the Arsenal captain and very quickly I came to understand that, to follow sport and become emotionally involved, you needed to withstand those two imposters, Triumph and Disaster.

The first year I followed the Gunners with any degree of comprehension, Arsenal beat Liverpool in the FA Cup Final. Lewis scored twice. It was not a pretty win. Early in the game Arsenal's flame-haired Scottish wing half Alex Forbes hacked down the flying Liverpool winger Billy Liddell who had to go off. A few years later, whenever I bought a take-away lunch from the Alex Forbes Sandwich Bar on the corner of Blackfriars Bridge – walking distance from the Hayters Sports Agency at Bridewell Place where I worked – I did so with just a smidgen of a guilty conscience.

But we won! That was the thing, we won. Not so the following year. Back at Wembley in another Cup Final, we lost the great Welsh full-back Walley Barnes to injury and went on to lose 1-0 to Newcastle United despite a heroic rear-guard action from goalie George Swindin, Laurie Smith, Ray Daniel and their colleagues. It was a ten man effort because there were no substitutes in those days. Afterwards, Joe Mercer said, "I thought captaining England was the highest honour I could achieve in the game. I was wrong. It was captaining Arsenal today." If the quote is not word perfect, the sentiment is. Mercer had just encapsulated the pride I felt in the team I had just discovered as a wide-eyed schoolboy.

Having already decided that Arsenal was the only team in the world worth worrying about because my cricketing hero Denis Compton played for them, I became indebted to my father for getting me to my first match. Harry Evans, a partner of Price Waterhouse, had been seconded to the Ministry of Supply during the war and, by chance, had come to know Sir Bracewell Smith who just happened to be Arsenal chairman at the time. He also knew another director, a Commander Bone.

So it was that I ended up in the Directors Box for that first visit when Arsenal beat Aston Villa 2-0 and I had the chance of meeting the goal scorer, Don Roper, afterwards when we were given a tour of the dressing rooms. It was heady stuff but I was soon back downstairs, paying my one shilling and sixpence to stand near the tunnel so as to get a close up view of my heroes as they trotted onto the pitch.

I did make one more visit to the Director's Box and grabbed the opportunity of taking my schoolboy friend, Nick Evans, who had taught me everything I knew about sport when I arrived at Seafield School at Cooden Beach in Sussex a year late. During my first term, I didn't know a right winger from a left back and had never heard of a googly. Nick and I were not related despite the co-incidental surname but were soon twinned in our love of sport. Being much better than me Nick went on to become a fine amateur footballer and cricketer and I am in his debt. He sowed the seeds of a life-long passion and I have tried never to hold his own affiliation against him. The poor fellow is a Spurs fan.

By the age of seventeen, I had done something about that passion and turned it into a career. Thanks to the inimitable Reg Hayter and his partners at the fledgling Hayters Sports Services – Ron Roberts and Freddie Garside – I was hired at a ridiculously young age and found myself reporting for all the major newspapers in Fleet Street as well as many in the provinces as Hayter's took in orders for match reports from all over the country.

It was a crash course in journalism and I cannot think a better one ever existed. Having to write three or even four reports on a match, all different to fit the style of each paper, in a freezing press box at 9.00 pm at night for, perhaps, the Times, Daily Express and Northampton Chronicle, dictating each one over a crackling phone to a copy taker while the grounds staff threatened to turn the lights out on you, made life working for a single newspaper, as I did later, an absolute d-d-doddle, as Reg would have called it.

It is nights at the Den, down Cold Blow Lane – such an apt name – that live most vividly in the memory although that may be coloured by the fact that it was there, covering one of Millwall's matches, that I actually met my hero. Denis Compton, retired from his exploits as a genius of a batsman for Middlesex and England, had turned to writing about football for the Sunday Express. After an introduction from Brian Glanville or John Camkin or whoever was there for that match, Compton turned to me and said, "Fancy a drink, old boy? I think we've earned it!". Writing for Denis was a lot more difficult than sending a perfect leg sweep to the boundary at Lord's so off we went to a local pub and I had stars in my eyes on the way home.

My career took me off on many different paths after that but I did get to cover matches at Highbury where, I hope, I managed to remove any Arsenal bias from my reporting. I have thrown myself more slack while writing this book because, quite unashamedly, I am writing from a fan's point of view with no sports editor demanding impartiality – a word that really does not exist in the vocabulary of a football fan.

Many decades later, I took a job as European Media Director for the Association of Tennis Professionals or the ATP as it is better known. They were opening a headquarters in Monaco which enabled me to take up residence in the Principality for a while without having to put the required half million pounds in your bank account. I took a flat in Fontvieille, about a hundred yards from Stade Louis II where AS Monaco play football. Slowly I became aware that there was a young manager working there who was, as the French say, 'pas comme les autres'.

It must have been in 1994 that I invited a new friend, David Dein and his wife Barbara to join me at the Monte Carlo Masters tennis tournament. As David then had a relatively modest yacht moored at Juan Les Pins – he has, I presume, a slightly bigger one now – he said he would sail it around to Monaco harbour and we should meet there. Having arranged transport to come to the port, I went round to pick them up and was invited on board for a drink.

"Do you mind if we wait a minute or two?" asked David. "I have this young Monaco manager dropping by for a quick chat. Very impressive fellow."

Almost immediately, the tall, elegant figure of Arsenal Wenger appeared quayside and went into a private huddle with David. As we drove to the tennis, Dein turned to me and said, "I think Arsene's the best young manager in the world."

So I was a lot less surprised than most when Wenger was unveiled as the new Arsenal manager in September 1996. It was a masterstroke on Dein's part and, of course, it began a managerial reign that transformed not only Arsenal Football Club, but the entire game in Britain as other managers, coaches and owners started to understand the Wenger Code.

So this has been an attempt, born out of frustration and bewilderment as much as anything, to chronicle the last of Arsenal's strange and unfulfilled seasons, not in the hope that I can discover the vital missing ingredient that can turn Wenger's nearly boys into winners but, at the very least, to lay out exactly what happened, the bad and the good, because, despite the headlines, there has been a lot of the latter, too.

I want to thank everyone who has helped me with the task, not least my energetic young agent, Melanie Michael-Greer, and my publisher Greg Adams, whose family's Arsenal connections as fans go back further than mine. And, then, of course there are numerous professional contacts, some of who wish to remain anonymous and, especially, those close to me who have put up with my need to be tied to a computer during long summer days. A setting in beautiful Buckinghamshire helped but, mostly, it was the encouragement of Ashley, my biggest supporter, that drove me towards a difficult deadline.

It has been written from the heart for those who love Arsenal and suffer, poor fools that we are, every time the Gunners misfire. How can a whole weekend be ruined because someone doesn't win a football match? I have no idea but it is. And there is no accounting for the spring in the step and the smile on the face when the net billows and a Dennis Bergkamp or Thierry Henry or a Theo Walcott wheels away and the final whistle blows and Arsenal have won. No accounting for it. Call it an obsession. A magnificent one, if you like, but it is real and it won't go away.

POSTSCRIPT

Twelve months earlier, five players had beaten the deadline on the night of August 31st and joined the club. This time, the minutes ticked away and Arsenal fans waited ......and waited. Nothing. Despite Arsene Wenger's assurances that he was still looking for "quality" players only a few days before, they did not materialize. In fact Wenger called off the chase so early that, on the final day, Arsenal were the only club to inform the Premier League that they would not be signing anyone. Efficient work by Ivan Gazidis' office but not quite what fans wanted to hear.

Andy Carroll went to West Ham on loan from Liverpool, who had nicked Real Madrid's Sahin on loan from under Arsenal's nose, and Clint Dempsey, who had wanted to go to Anfield, ended up at Tottenham who had just sold Van der Vaart to Hamburg.

So with Podolski, Giroud and Cazorla secured long before, Arsenal - having shipped out the likes of Nicklas Bendtner on loan to Juventus - were left with a tidy little profit of £10.3 million in transfer dealings for the summer. Many fans were apoplectic. And not just because Van Persie and Song had gone.

A few days before the deadline, it appeared that Theo Walcott might be joining them. Walcott had one year left on his contract and Wenger rarely allowed a situation like this to rest. Either the player was re-signed to a long term contract, as had been the case with Thomas Vermaelen and Laurent Koscielny, or they were sold while there was still money to be made – like the £24 million gathered in from Van Persie.

The word on Walcott was that it was all about money, with the club refusing to offer more than £75,000 a week. Echoes of an agent's urging were apparent once again. But Wenger quickly stepped in to refute that suggestion, backing up the assertion of Mick Dennis in the Daily Express that "in the fickle world of football fandom, the truth is far more nuanced than the supporters acknowledge."

Nuance. It's not a word you hear too frequently at football stadiums across the country and even less when people are considering the merits of Walcott. Despite having enjoyed his best ever season, there were still those who thought him a poor crosser of a ball and a poor decision maker. Statistics suggested otherwise and, had he gone, Arsenal would have lost the three players who had dominated the goals and assists columns in 2011-2012 – Van Persie, Song and Walcott.

But Theo stayed – at least in the short term. He met with Wenger and, apparently, expressed frustration at a wage package of something around £75,000 a week. Ridiculous, really, that any 23-year-old should be complaining about being a millionaire but that's what happens when other, only marginally better, players are paid £120,000 a week and up.

Wenger, who has a genuine affection for this well mannered young man, explained in detail. "It was never a hard-line approach," he said. "Always a soft-line approach with respect to our pay structure. In every decision we have a general line of conduct that is our wage structure and we want to respect it. It is, of course, different for a 29-year-old and a 23-year-old. Theo is not money obsessed. He does not say 'It's that or not.' There are little differences in negotiation that can happen. But I think Theo loves the club and he will continue to play for us."

Then Arsene came up with one of those remarks that leaves the world of football managerdom, to borrow from Dennis, and enters the philosophical. "We still have not found a machine that can measure the intensity of love," he said. "We would all buy it."

And make it part of the Wenger Code.

Writing in the Independent, Jack Pitt-Brooke reflected that Wenger was "still trying to operate in the pre-billionaire era, hoping decency, stability, and a tight wage structure will be enough to keep his favourites."

It was precisely what the manager had been doing ever since he arrived in London but times had changed. Oligarchs had moved, if not onto his manor, then onto some uncomfortably adjacent. But there were still moments to savour and one came when Chelsea went down to Monaco to play at the Stade Louis II, where Arsene used to work, and lost 4-1 to Atletico Madrid in the SuperCup. Chelsea's oligarch had just spent £80 million on bringing new players to the club.

Wenger's observation was acute. "Spending itself is not a quality. Buying good players is a quality; buying better players than you already have is a quality."

So how well did our parsimonious manager buy in the least active summer Arsenal had indulged in throughout their Premier League history?

On the evidence of the first three matches, not badly at all. After two 0-0 draws against Sunderland and Stoke City, Wenger took the team up to Anfield where a new manager, Brendan Rodgers was fuming over his own transfer dealings. Having loaned out Carroll to West Ham on the understanding that the club's American owners would allow him to bring in replacements, he had been left high and dry with nothing resembling a centre forward.

The result was that Arsenal kept their third clean sheet – evidence that Steve Bould was having an effect on the back four – while up front Cazorla and Podolski started to weave a little magic. The Spaniard found the German for the first goal and, in the second half it was Podolski who found Cazorla. Santi's power-driven shot went in off his mate Reina's left elbow. The Liverpool goalie was criticized for that but, earlier, he had saved brilliantly from the dangerous Gibbs and he just got a trifle unlucky with the Cazorla goal.

It mattered not. Arsenal came away with a 2-0 win and only Van Persie's hat-trick at Southampton, his last two goals coming in the 88th and 92nd minutes to save Manchester United who had been trailing 1-2, soured the weekend. Would Van Persie go on to do something almost unique and have an even better season after leaving Arsenal than he had enjoyed at the Emirates?

It was one of the questions Arsenal fans were pondering as word started reaching us from Barcelona that Cesc Fabregas was beginning to get itchy feet. He was being subbed too much, he told a local radio station. He wanted to play more.

Unlike Flamini, Hleb, Henry and to a lesser extent Nasri and Clichy, Fabregas had enjoyed a very successful first season at Barcelona but now reality was starting to sink in. There were players called Iniesta and Xavi above him in the pecking order. And they wouldn't make way.

No doubt Cesc found time to discuss all this with his great pal, Danny Karbassiyoon, Arsenal's chief scout in North America, who had just spent the weekend with him in Barcelona. Time to talk about the merits and de-merits of leaving a club like Arsenal, which, for the majority of players, has turned out to be a not very good idea.

How long that will last remains to be seen. The new cap on what big clubs are allowed to spend comes into force very soon now and that, we hope, will force the oligarchs to fall back to a spending line that will be closer to the financial aspects of the Wenger Code. Then, perhaps, no one will be able to lure players away with ludicrous offers of £180,000 a week and Arsene will be able to enjoy the fruits of his labours to the full.

But don't expect it all to make sense. We have seen how strong is the strain of illogicality which runs through football and, added to that is something Wenger picked up on with one of those off-the-cuff observations that always make him worth listening to.

"We have moved from a thinking society to an emotional society," he said, the rants of his critics no doubt ringing in his ears. "And we have to live with that."

We most certainly do and all we can hope for is that thought, intelligent thought, can still have an influence on deed. The emotion will automatically follow.

INDEX

INDEX

INDEX

INDEX

**ARSENAL INDEPENDENT
SUPPORTERS' ASSOCIATION**

AISA was formed on Sunday 1st October 2000, hours before Thierry Henry's 'wonder goal' at Highbury that led to a 1-0 victory over Manchester United. Over 50 supporters attended the inaugural meeting at St. Paul's Road, London N1. **AISA**'s membership, including associate members, has since grown to over 8,000, making it by far the largest Arsenal supporters club.

The main objects of **AISA** are to:

- Represent and campaign on behalf of Arsenal supporters.
- Organise high quality services for **AISA** members.
- Promote the history, values and traditions of Arsenal Football Club.
- Encourage the Directors and Management of Arsenal Football Club to appreciate, welcome and value the support and participation of all Arsenal fans.

AISA believes that fans' views and experiences should be at the centre of the Club's decision-making process. We work co-operatively with other Arsenal supporters organisations to keep supporters' views at the forefront.

AISA campaigns on issues such as improving the atmosphere, providing better catering arrangements, the stewarding and policing operations, transport to and from the stadium. We meet regularly with the Club's chief executive, and with various other Arsenal senior managers and directors.

Everything we do is informed by our members, through their feedback, and by fans in general through regular surveys and various other formal and informal tools.

AISA has developed a charity fundraising programme, mainly supporting the Arsenal charity of the season, which has raised over £70,000 in the last 5 years.

Following the 2011 change in the ownership of the Club we continue to campaign against debt being secured against the club and the raising of short-term profits through significant increases in ticket prices.

AISA has a number of important relationships with external organisations, notably Islington Borough Council and the Islington Police as well as Delaware North, Arsenal's catering supplier.

Every Arsenal supporter is welcome to join AISA. We have members as young as 8 and others well into their 80s. Many members attend matches every week, others are not so lucky but support the team in every way they can. AISA is based in Islington but our members live in every part of the UK, and in over 40 other countries.

Membership fees are minimal; join at www.aisa.org or write to AISA, PO Box 65011, London N5 9AX. For more information email us at info@aisa.org.

The Arsenal Supporters' Trust exists to bring together Shareholders and Supporters of Arsenal Football Club.

Our goal is to ensure an element of supporter ownership, representation and influence is maintained at Arsenal in the years ahead. Large numbers of our members are already personal Arsenal shareholders.

In August 2010 Arsenal Fanshare was launched to facilitate mutual ownership of Arsenal shares. **www.arsenalfanshare.com**

Every member of the Trust shares in ownership of Arsenal Football Club through the shares the Trust owns.

The Trust works with its members, Arsenal executives, the club's Board, major shareholders and other Arsenal supporter groups to help build Arsenal into a world class sporting institution.

Arsenal is a name and a club already widely admired around the football world. Together we can take it to even greater heights, both on and off the field. The Arsenal tradition is one of ground-breaking innovation. Please join us and support our work.

As well as holding monthly board meetings which members are welcome to attend, the Trust holds special events for its membership. In recent seasons, these have included an annual Q&A session with the managing director/CEO of the club, a Christmas drinks social in Arsenal's exclusive Diamond Club, a tour of the stadium's press facilities and a meeting for members with relevant ministers at the Houses of Parliament.

For details of how to join, visit our website at
www.arsenaltrust.org